LIVING IN THE SLIPSTREAM

LIVING IN THE SLIPSTREAM

Compiled by Jill Black, Holly Jeffers,
and Alison Bairsto

Book Guild Publishing
Sussex, England

First published in Great Britain in 2014 by
The Book Guild Ltd
The Werks
45 Church Road
Hove, BN3 2BE

Typesetting in Garamond by
Norman Tilley Graphics Ltd, Northampton

Printed and bound in Great Britain by
CPI Group (UK) Ltd, Croydon, CR0 4YY

A catalogue record for this book is available from
The British Library.

ISBN 978 1 909716 24 7

Contents

Foreword

This collection of personal and amusing memories by RAF Wives is not only a great read, but also is in support of two very important charities; The Royal Air Forces Association and The Royal Air Force Benevolent Fund.

Having been an RAF wife myself, albeit for a short time compared to many of the authors of these stories, it is interesting to read about some of these situations reflecting all aspects of RAF life over the last fifty years.

I loved my time in Anglesey when William was serving with RAF Search and Rescue. I cannot pretend that I didn't feel anxious at times when William was on shift in howling gales, knowing that he was out flying in extremely challenging conditions, but he loved doing it and I always felt incredibly proud of him. I also knew that I was not alone and that there were many supportive Search and Rescue wives on Anglesey and at other bases across the country.

'Living in the Slipstream' is an extraordinary collection of anecdotes that have been brilliantly put together. I would like to congratulate Jill, Alison and Holly for their efforts supporting the excellent work of Royal Air Force Charities. These stories are part of the RAF's story, and this book gives us all a chance to celebrate them.

Catherine.

Acknowledgements

Alison, Jill and Holly would like to thank the following people for their help in producing this book:

Her Royal Highness The Duchess of Cambridge for her warm and sincere Foreword.

Our story contributors, more than 100 of them, who have given up their time and have shared their funny and sometimes poignant memories to record a snapshot of RAF history. Without them there would be no book.

Maggie May, an author herself, who has kindly written a new poem, 'They Might Have Told Us', especially for us.

Trevor Benneworth RAAF, who has given us permission to reprint 'Ode to an Airforce Wife'.

Our three husbands, who have encouraged and supported us throughout the venture.

Kate Black, for a very patient extended photography session.

Al Turner MBE, our cartoonist, who has cleverly illustrated the front cover and captured a number of the stories in his own inimitable way. He has suffered from MS for several years and is now confined to a wheelchair, but despite having the use of only one hand, has produced some wonderful cartoons and managed to capture the essence of the stories brilliantly.

Preface and Reflections

THE COLD WAR

Recent military activity has involved our armed forces operating in areas far from home, including Iraq and Afghanistan, requiring them to maintain a mobile capability for deployment anywhere in the world. We forget that from 1961 when the Berlin Wall was erected, to 1989 when it was demolished, our armed forces prepared for a very different war; a static war over the whole of mainland Europe where NATO forces faced those of the USSR and its Eastern Bloc allies. As one side developed a capability, including nuclear weapons, it was quickly matched by the other until vast armies, navies and air forces faced each other across the borders of the western world from north to south.

This period of some thirty years after World War II was known as the Cold War, and many of the tales and anecdotes in this book are told by Air Force wives who were caught up in that confrontation as their husbands prepared to combat the very real threat posed by the Soviet Union.

This short explanation is important in order to understand much of the jargon and many of the abbreviations used in several of the stories. Two in particular stand out: QRA and Battle Flight. Quick Reaction Alert involved a small number of our aircraft being held at readiness, fully armed and fully manned by crews able to get airborne within minutes – the bombers to attack Soviet targets and the fighters to defend against Soviet bombers. Typically, aircraft on QRA had to be airborne within ten minutes. Battle Flight was the equivalent force in Germany held by the fighters but, because they were based only thirty-five miles from the East German border, they had to be airborne within five minutes.

QRA and Battle Flight usually involved two aircraft positioned in small hangarettes at the end of a runway. They were fully armed and ready to scramble instantly. The aircrew and groundcrew were normally on duty for twenty-four hours, and on Battle Flight the aircrew would sleep in their flying kit in order to maintain their five-minute state of readiness. Aircraft on both QRA and Battle Flight were scrambled almost daily throughout the Cold War in response to Soviet activity spotted on their side of the border. Although very necessary, QRA and Battle Flight placed a huge burden on the squadrons who held it, and was much disliked by aircrew and groundcrew alike (and by their wives whose husbands could disappear for days at a time). Spare a thought, therefore, for the Typhoon crews who continue to hold QRA in the Falklands today.

REFLECTIONS

Jill

It is easy to forget that when my husband joined the RAF in 1965 it was only twenty years since the end of the Second World War, and that when we were married three years later in 1968 the RAF was still very much a male-orientated club. Rank, privilege and status counted for everything and everyone was expected to toe the line without question or favour. Collecting and writing some of these tales has reminded me of the good times, the fun and the laughter we had as a family following 'in the slipstream' of the RAF. It was certainly a different era in those days, and RAF wives had to put up with a lot.

I never realised before getting married that I would not be able to follow my own career, that I would have to move house twenty-six times, that my children would have to go to boarding school, that I would be left on my own for weeks at a time, that my husband would be sent to war, that we would lose many good friends through aircraft accidents, and that I would be constantly on edge in case one day it might be my own husband. It always annoyed me that on every holiday my husband could not wait to get back to his squadron for fear of missing out on his beloved flying, and I really resented being referred to as 'Wife of …'.

However, these things aside, we were given opportunities and experiences beyond the wildest dreams of most of our civilian friends, and I hope others find as much humour and pleasure in reading these stories as we did in putting them together.

Alison

Collating stories from friends and other RAF wives has been an interesting experience. It has awoken hitherto forgotten memories and made me reflect on my time as an RAF wife. Looking at our collection it would appear that we led a very privileged existence and a life full of tea and buns – nothing could be further from the truth, but like childbirth I think we have all managed to remember the glorious parts and forget the heartache, loneliness, irritation and fear that often accompanied our lives. Moving constantly, never living in your 'own' home, children in boarding school, far away from family, absent husbands on exercise or at war, no career, permanently changing jobs, a CV that most employers shuddered to see, leaving pets behind, all these played their part in our lives. But on the upside we had a very varied and interesting life, we saw places and did things that few others ever get the chance to, we made hundreds of acquaintances and some very special friends who supported us in the most bizarre range of emergencies, we developed independence, enjoyed a community spirit and, for the most part, we had fun.

My daughter and son-in-law are both in the RAF now, as a doctor and a pilot respectively. It has been refreshing to know that the professionalism, camaraderie, and fun still exist, but they are in a different Air Force. It is much smaller, the demands are different and both have been on active service from the outset of their careers. The patriarchal society we once enjoyed no longer exists. Life does not revolve around the 'married patch', most young people live in their own homes and commute, the Officers' Mess is a shadow of its former self – you can't even get a coffee from a machine there nowadays, let alone be served by an attentive steward. Young wives are likely to have their own career and may even be the primary earner; they do not follow blindly. Communications are infinitely better and it is more a job than the total way of life that we experienced.

However, they still need our help and the help of our wonderful RAF charities such as RAFA and The Benevolent Fund. My daughter experienced this first hand: husband in Afghanistan, she had to be on call for a month at Brize Norton with two hours' notice to move to collect casualties from across the world, usually a minimum of a forty-eight-hour trip. Where do you live and who looks after the baby? Thankfully three charities have refurbished and fitted out a small number of surplus married quarters which were able to become our temporary home. Grannie, of course, had to do the baby sitting – the Royal Air Force still hasn't quite recognised that its womenfolk may also be mothers!

During the time we were in Brize Norton, my daughter's husband was due to return from his six-month tour in Afghanistan – sadly my daughter flew out to the same destination to collect a casualty the night before he landed, their flight paths probably crossed. On returning from war he was met not by his adoring wife but by his mother-in-law – the blow was softened a little as his baby son took his first steps and gave him a rapturous welcome.

Holly

It has been a privilege to have been involved in the compilation of these stories and to have read the personal memories of wives who were, without doubt, the supreme 'camp followers'. Their tales give a fascinating glimpse into a social/military history, narrow in its field and generally not appreciated in the civilian world.

Readers might be surprised to find so much fun, frivolity and humour in these cameos, which cover the period from the 1950s onwards. Being able to see the lighter side of life, and actually living it, compensated for those inevitable periods of anxiety, stress and grief. This is a largely bygone era, when fortitude and the 'get on with it' spirit still prevailed. Life on a bleak airfield under the heavy cloud of the Cold War was not easy, while the difficulties of moving abroad, or simply living 'behind the wire', presented their own problems. These wives were the ultimate home-makers who could, at the drop of a hat, convert damp and dreary quarters into cosy homes for their husbands and children. It is hard to convey the atmosphere of those pre hi-tech days or to make comparisons with family life in the modern Royal Air Force. So much has changed over the past five or six decades.

As the manuscript of this book neared its completion, I was left wondering who had vacated all of those less-than-clean quarters, when it seems our writers had all handed theirs over in immaculate order!

1

Joining the Slipstream

ODE TO AN AIR FORCE WIFE

It was never said by an Air Force wife
That variety is the spice of life,
The poor thing never knows where she's at
As home is wherever he hangs his hat.

She lives in a quarter, often large and commodious,
But with walls and carpets in colours quite odious,
And she cannot bring in her favourite chair
As it clashes with curtains, already there.
And the garden is vast, damp and forlorn
The vegetable patch has more grass than the lawn.

She moves every year into new married quarters
In the meantime bearing his sons and his daughters.
He always goes first – to find quarter or hiring
While she's left behind for the cleaning and ironing.
And during the move, isn't it strange
How the kids all catch measles and the dog gets mange.

The new house may be small with no room for expansion
Or it may be a flat or a hut or a mansion.
But she left her place spotless – her successors so lucky,
So why is the new place so incredibly mucky?
She must scrub and tidy all over again

Accept calls from neighbours between labour pains.
To think last year she'd servants and lived like a lady
While now she's a skivvy and has a new baby.

Now his house must be run like a club or hotel
He brings friends in at all hours – strangers as well
And with no time to settle she must dress up pretty
And go to the mess all charming and witty,
And dance with young officers noisy and clamorous
And with their seniors, decrepit and amorous.

She must drink the concoctions, punch or beer
Moderately of course or she'll wreck his career
She is bored and exhausted – I am stuck for a rhyme
While he's in the bar having a helluva time.

At the age to retire he's still handsome and hearty
Elegant and charming, the life of a party.
She is worn and haggard, cranky and nervous.
An absolute wreck after thirty years' service.

But even so when all's said and done,
She still believes service life is such fun,
She has roughed it throughout but really, good grief,
She'd have been bored to death with a business chief.

A FOREIGN COUNTRY

The Air Commodore's wife reminded me a little of Mr Darcy's aunt, the formidable Lady Catherine de Bourgh. It was her duty, as she saw it, to maintain standards in society; to ensure that newcomers knew their place in that society and to engage, with great condescension, in charitable works for lesser mortals. As a newly arrived lesser mortal, I was currently the object of her charity and her advice. 'My dear, you are a new bride. Allow me to guide you. Now, first of all – have you ordered your calling cards?'

When I look back I find it truly incredible that I once inhabited an Air Force world where calling cards were deemed necessary. Thank the lord, a young Squadron Leader's wife took pity on me and told me that calling cards were no longer required and not to waste any money on them. But I was within an inch of ordering hundreds and they would no doubt still be languishing unused in some trunk, along with the remains of the 'At Home' invitations that I ordered by the ton ('Engraved, my dear, not printed').

My husband's first posting was as a junior medical officer at the Royal Air Force College at Cranwell and I'm not sure if the fact that it was Cranwell was a good thing or not; had we gone straight to a front-line station my first experience of Air Force life would have been much less formal and much less prescriptive. However, I would not have caught the tail end of a dying era in service life, or experienced a set of rules for wives that was already considered old-fashioned elsewhere in the RAF but was still enshrined at Cranwell. Looking back, I'm glad that I spent some time in a world that now seems as foreign as an Edwardian period drama, or like some tale of the Raj where senior officers' wives kept the barbarians at bay. And yet, astonishingly, this was only 40 years ago.

I was newly married and desperately keen to do the right thing, so I threw myself into this new world: I called on the Commandant's wife at the prescribed time (even though I didn't leave my calling card); I joined the Wives' Club, faithfully attending every meeting and even rising to the exalted position of secretary; I invited the Senior Medical Officer's wife to tea (best china cups and saucers, although I lost points for not having a lemon-squeezer for the Earl Grey); I helped out at the Thrift Shop; I learned to give Sherry Mornings (a singularly pointless type of entertaining which left you ravenously hungry before lunchtime and mildly tipsy for the whole of the afternoon, but without having had a proper conversation with anyone). Soon, however, I saw where real power lay and I realised that I was ill-equipped to grasp that power: I

Sherry mornings!

hadn't been asked to join the rota for doing Mess Flowers! Four years spent studying for a degree in English Literature was of little worth if I didn't know how to soak my Oasis. So I even went to flower-arranging classes (without much success – at one point I thought my husband's career was blighted for ever when my pedestal had to be taken to bits and redone by a more skilful practitioner).

I really wanted to do the right thing and I worked hard at it. But the one thing it never occurred to me to do was to go out and get a proper job. That would have been practically unthinkable – in those days officers' wives did not work. Not only that, wives of Squadron Leaders and above were given help in the house in the form of 'batting': an anachronism from the days when an officer was assigned a batman as his personal servant. To reinforce the image of an Edwardian 'Upstairs, Downstairs' world, at Cranwell the batting was carried out mainly by airmen's wives keen to supplement the family income. A familiar sight at Cranwell, first thing every morning as the inevitable mist was clearing, was a line of wives crossing the North Airfield from the airmen's married quarters to the officers' patch to start work. Could you conceive of such a thing happening today?

'The past is a foreign country.' We revisit it with a mixture of horror and amusement; so easy to mock. And yet there was a sense of social cohesion and a support network which should not be mocked. Those formidable senior officers' wives made sure that, in a crisis or an emergency, no one was abandoned: a husband on an overseas detachment could be sure that his wife would be looked after; the mother of a sick child knew that her other children would be cared for if she had to spend time in hospital; the Thrift Shop was a thriving concern in rural Lincolnshire (and ahead of its time now that charity shops are seen as a source of vintage clothing).

After only fourteen months we were posted to Germany, and the world I left behind at Cranwell soon seemed just as foreign as the next overseas posting. I can laugh at myself now for having thought that it all mattered, but some things I learned were worthwhile. I've never been very good at flower arranging but at least, if I'm asked to help decorate the local church for Christmas or Harvest Festival, I know how to soak my Oasis.

ADVICE FOR AN AIR FORCE WIFE-TO-BE

I was newly engaged and visiting my fiancé's parents. My future father-in-law was a very senior RAF officer. On arrival at their home we were greeted with tea in the drawing room, and then the lecture began.

I had to understand that while I might think I was marrying the man of my dreams and that I would be centre of his universe and the constant focus of his attention, in reality he was already married to the Royal Air Force and I would always come a very lowly second. His career must come first; I must not put any demands on him or question the system, and must just take what came along, supporting him in every possible way. He would most likely prefer spending most of his time in the Mess with his fellow officers where he would be provided with sumptuous meals and immaculate service. Home cooking, not to mention creature comforts, were an irrelevance. The Royal Air Force had all claims on his time and I should never question his absence or even his whereabouts. Even though I was a graduate, I should not consider progressing my own career or even taking a job, as I now had a new life ahead of me as a Royal Air Force Officer's Wife.

We were duly married and I had great delight when, on my parents-in-law's first visit to us, my husband was unexpectedly diverted for most of the weekend. I dutifully explained (with tongue in cheek) that, of course, they would understand – Air Force commitments had to come first!

ONE BEETLE AND NEWLY MARRIED

In 1969, all we possessed was a VW Beetle, a couple of suitcases and a trunk full of wedding presents on the roof-rack. As a new young wife in the RAF I did not exist! My husband and I were both 22 years old and considered far too young to get married. Marriage was not recognised in those days for anyone under 25 years of age. We had to pay my fare to RAF Gutersloh in Germany, which seemed a million miles away, and we didn't qualify for a Married Quarter.

So, with my newly qualified Lightning pilot husband about to join his first squadron, we set off from the UK on New Year's Day with our worldly possessions on the roof of the car. After an arduous journey through snow and ice we finally got to the outskirts of Gutersloh and I dared to ask where we were going to live. 'Oh, the squadron will find us somewhere,' was the reply.

We eventually arrived at the squadron and I was told to wait in the car, in freezing conditions, wondering what on earth I had got myself into. I was chilled to the bone when my husband finally returned, after what seemed like hours, having been introduced to the 'chaps'. He had some good news about accommodation. Someone knew of a one-bedroom flat that was available on the other side of Gutersloh. We drove down winding lanes in the middle of nowhere to a barn in a field. This was to be my first home. The 'flat' was in the eaves of the barn above the cows, and the smell was dreadful. We unpacked our belongings and retired for the night, thoroughly exhausted.

Then, at some time shortly after midnight, we were woken by the sound of loud banging on the door. One of those interminable Cold War exercises had been called. I was later to discover that this was an almost weekly event, which occurred at any time of the day or night on weekdays, weekends, high days and holidays, and that, when called, my husband would disappear instantly. And so it was on this occasion. He took off into the night with the car, a fellow squadron member and barely a goodbye.

As dawn broke I found myself alone in the roof of a barn, freezing cold, miles from anywhere and without a car. The electricity had gone off and there was no phone to call for help. This was the beginning of my Air Force life.

My only way to keep warm was to stay in bed. This was not a particular problem but after a day and a night on my own, and fast running out of books, it was becoming seriously tedious. The following day I was saved by the arrival of a fellow squadron wife whose first comment on entering the flat was, 'What on earth is that smell?'

'Cows,' I replied.

She had been married at least two months longer than me and seemed to know the ropes. 'Don't worry,' she said. 'The men will be gone a long time, then, once the exercise is over, there will be a beer call and goodness knows how long that will last.' However, she had a car and I could at last get out of the flat. Life began to look up.

UNDER TWENTY-FIVE

As I approached my wedding day, in apple blossom time during the late 1960s, I couldn't have been more excited. Not only was I to marry the man with whom I had fallen in love, a newly qualified pilot who had just joined his first squadron as a Vulcan co-pilot, but I was to begin a whole new life.

My single days were almost over and my career in 'swinging London' would be exchanged for a military life in Cyprus. What a prospect! For the icing on the (wedding) cake my new parents-in-law had presented us with tickets to spend our honeymoon on a cruise ship. We would board the SS *Apollonia*, a Greek vessel, in Marseille in the south of France. Then we would sail all the way to Limassol on the romantic island of Cyprus, via numerous exotic Mediterranean ports.

There was a reason behind this most generous of wedding presents, for my prospective husband and I were only 22 years old – under the magic age of 25, the full significance of which would become very clear to me later. It was just not done in those days to be married before that age, and my fiancé had done his duty and formally presented himself in front of his Squadron Commander to ask permission to wed. The CO's unconsidered response was, 'No. Absolutely not! I was thirty eight when I got married … and I married a 21-year-old dollybird. You, a young Flying Officer, just starting out in your career, have more important things to concentrate on.' This was a bit of blow for my beloved and, with a dismissive gesture, the CO then added, 'You don't qualify for any allowances yet, remember.'

In common with many other young couples of that time, we went ahead anyway, unconcerned and unworried. So I had bought myself a new wardrobe of summer clothes and was anticipating a wonderful honeymoon cruise. Apparently, if we had been older, I could have 'indulged' to Akrotiri on a Britannia transport aircraft. That meant nothing to me at the time – my RAF knowledge was pretty rudimentary.

Many of my belongings, including a beautiful matching pair of bedside lamps, had already been taken to RAF Waddington where they were transported in a Vulcan bomb bay to Cyprus. I had been anxiously awaiting news of my new home, and it wasn't until almost the last minute that my fiancé had secured a flat. 'It's brand new … with a great view across the bay to RAF Akrotiri. You will be able to watch the aircraft taking off and landing!' How exciting. Everything was ready.

Three weeks later we were showered with confetti as we disembarked onto a tender off Limassol – there was no harbour in those days. The crew navigator was on the seafront to welcome us and transport us to our new home in the little village of Polemedia. My new husband gallantly insisted on carrying me across the threshold. It was all very romantic and he was so thrilled to show me the flat that he had taken so much trouble to find. There was a nice little kitchen, with a clever louvered glass window looking out to the sea view he had spoken of, a large sitting room, a dining room and vast hall, plus two bedrooms and a bathroom with black floor tiles. Perfect. But as I gazed around I realised that it contained minimal furniture, in fact practically none.

The spare bedroom was absolutely empty. Our bedroom looked quite spacious with its double bed and one chest of drawers; nothing to put my new lamps on. A three-piece suite stood alone in the lounge, and the modern teak table and its two matching chairs dominated the dining room.

'Why only two chairs?' I enquired gently.

'Ah, I thought you might ask,' my husband replied. 'Uhm. Well – that's all I could afford.'

'You've bought them, then?'

'Uh, well no. Actually, I had to rent them.'

'What do you mean, rent?'

'Well, it's what they do here. The crew took me down to Limassol to this Greek guy called Papadopoulos. It's where we get things.'

'Goodness!' I hardly knew what to say. 'So I can go and choose some more things then?' I was thinking about some nice chests for my bedside lamps.

'Darling, I'm afraid that is all we can afford.' He looked truly crestfallen. Then he brightened. 'We shall be much better off when we get marriage allowance. But that will probably not be for about two years – then we'll be posted!'

LOVE'S YOUNG DREAM

Arriving on my first operational RAF station in the early 1970s, I soon found myself bowled over and engaged to one of the fighter squadron's 'eligible' bachelors. As a member of the Air Traffic Control team, it was deemed a good idea for me to get airborne to experience our services from the aircrew's point of view so, after much discussion, I was given the CO's permission to fly with my fiancé. I was soon off to the Flying Clothing Section to be kitted out and there the banter from numerous fighter pilots began, as they too prepared for their flights.

How mad was I to agree to fly in this aircraft?

Did I not know that it leaked like a sieve? You can't have missed seeing the trays placed underneath to catch the fuel and oil drips?

And what about how it hated the rain and was prone to all kinds of electrical failures?

I pondered all these comments carefully before my tormentors' conversation turned to asking which of the squadron pilots I was going to fly with. I confidently and lovingly named him, provoking screams of laughter and many derogatory remarks about his flying skills and attitude to life in general.

As I recovered from this, my engagement ring was then noticed and duly remarked upon. 'So who is the lucky feller?' I leave it to the reader's imagination to consider the reaction to my very tentative reply!

POSTAL FAUX PAS

When I was a young wife, whose native tongue was not English, my husband (not known for his tact and diplomacy; we'd say 'political correctness' these days) was sent on detachment to the Far East for three months. He had arranged to send me the house-keeping money every month by cheque through the post (BFPO).

After a week or two alone with two small children, I decided that

11

we would all go and stay with my parents in the Netherlands for a few weeks. My husband continued to send me a monthly cheque through the Forces Post Office, but none of them was forwarded to me in Holland. In fact, for the whole of his detachment, I received nothing. In the meantime I had to 'sponge' off my parents, who were saying, 'Told you so – he's gone off and left you.'

Eventually it was sorted out and all my money came at once! The children and I returned to our quarter at Honington.

During that time, the Squadron Commander's wife held a little coffee morning for the wives whose husbands were still out in the Far East. During the conversation she asked me if I had heard from my beloved, so I told her that it had taken nearly two months before I even received a letter from him. I went on to tell her that my husband had said it was the 'wogs' who had been holding up the post – believing that was slang for the people who worked in the postal service! There was a rattling of coffee cups and saucers followed by a pregnant silence. I can't remember now who explained that what I had said was not really ladylike. I soon learned not to repeat some of the words my husband used.

PVC BOOTS

We had only been married for two weeks when my new husband had to go on Battle Flight (5 minutes readiness to fly) for 24 hours.

We were living out in a village called Reitburg in the German countryside and it was exactly 11 miles to the RAF base. Towards the end of his standby duty I thought what a nice idea it would be to go and meet him – but I had never in my life walked as many as 11 miles. Never mind, I put on my most practical footwear – a pair of black PVC knee-high boots, and off I went. It was quiet, hardly anyone about and I only saw two cars. One of them slowed right down and the driver said something to me in German, but I didn't understand a word and he drove on. Perhaps he was negotiating a price?

Eventually I reached the main road between the top married quarters and the bottom patch, and by now was expecting to see my weary husband driving back. There was no sign of him. I did notice a couple from 19 Squadron who were obviously collecting their Sunday papers. They must have passed me three times before they finally stopped and offered me a lift. They'd noticed me walking and thought that seemed a bit strange. I gratefully accepted the lift and they kindly took me to Battle Flight where I was reunited with my husband. If I hadn't been rescued I wouldn't have made it, because I'd completely forgotten my ID!

When we eventually got home, my husband had to cut off my lovely boots because I had the most horrendous blisters. For the next week I had to sleep with a cardboard box over my feet to protect them from our heavy blankets!

DUTCH STEAK

Very soon after we married (back in the early 1960s), while my husband was serving on a Canberra Strike Squadron at RAF Bruggen, we managed to find accommodation in Holland, my home country just across the border near Roermond. You will appreciate that there were no married quarters or hirings available for under 25s in those days. We had had a fairly short courtship, my English was very limited, and we were still discovering the joys of married life and learning some of the 'cultural' differences between our countries of origin.

At 21 years of age, although not an experienced cook, I was desperate to impress my new spouse with my culinary expertise. In passing one day I asked him if he fancied horse meat. He was adamant that he did not and that he really didn't want even to give it a try, so I let matters rest for a few weeks. Then one day, while shopping at the local village butcher, I spied some very nice-looking steaks (horse, of course) and thought they looked so much like beef that he wouldn't know the difference. So I bought a couple and decided to serve them to him for our evening meal. He was then due to set off for Bruggen to take over on QRA (Quick Reaction Alert; 10 minutes readiness to fly) for 24 hours. He remarked how tender and tasty they were and asked if I would be going back to the same butcher sometime. 'Yes, sure,' I said and then made the mistake of asking him if he realised he had just eaten his first horse meat. He was hopping mad, stormed out the house (actually a tiny bungalow) and headed off to work in a huge huff!

We had no phone in those days, and I couldn't drive, so there was no way I could contact him to see if he had calmed down or come to terms with his unwelcome experience. I really thought that that was the end of our marriage. To this day, if I try serving anything he doesn't immediately recognise he asks, 'Is that horsemeat?'

RED ARROWS: THEN THERE WERE NINE

At last I'd finally got the hang of finding my way around the Isle of Anglesey without a map. One day I set out on my new motor-bike from our flat above that popular 'out-of-hours' hostelry the Rhosneigr Club, and found my way home some time later happy and content with my achievement. Life was good. But that evening my husband returned from work very excited. He soon announced that there was a plan afoot to increase the number of the Red Arrows from seven to nine aircraft, and that we were off to the Cotswolds to join them in the hope that he might become the first Red 9.

Funny how one's mind works at times like that. I thought about having to leave all the new friends we had just made in the short time we had been there, about giving up the horse that I had found to ride, about the effort I had put into making our first home so cheerful and cosy, about the wonderful beach and cliff walks that would no longer be possible, and suddenly realised that this lovely lifestyle we had created for ourselves was about to be gone for ever. It was quite usual in the RAF to have to move every two years or so, and we all expected it. But to be told we were moving after only two months, having just set up our first marital home together, was something of a surprise and should have warned me what to expect as an RAF wife!

However, like riding my new motorbike, I quickly changed gear and found myself caught up in the excitement of the move and of the new life ahead. After all, I thought, with only nine team members it would take no time at all to get to know everyone, and we'd no longer have to put up with the cigarette smoke that came up through our bedroom floorboards from the bar below!

'There they go again,' I thought to myself as the 9-ship swooped past my window for the umpteenth time, while I was firmly grounded at the kitchen sink. How long before they return this time I wondered? I knew the team would be displaying at RNAS Culdrose in the near future, and suddenly a trip to Cornwall seemed like a great idea. So, come the day of the air show, my sister-in-law and I set off in separate cars for the naval air station – unfortunately forgetting that many of the locals and most of the county's holidaymakers would be doing the same thing. It wasn't long before we found ourselves in one of those deep sunken Cornish lanes, nose-to-tail in traffic, with no hope of arriving in time for the thrill of the display.

Then the moment came that changed the whole expedition: Red 9 appeared from nowhere and flew directly over my car, completely distracting me. The next thing I knew I had crashed into the back of my sister-in-law's ancient van and, although I didn't know it at the time, shunted her into a brand new Triumph Spitfire. I spent the rest of the afternoon in the local police station, with a bloody knee, pondering the cost of it all, and realising that being a Red Arrows camp-follower was not going to be as straightforward as I had thought.

THE ADC'S WIFE

It all happened very fast. He proposed in the September and the date was set for December. Three months, plenty of time to organise a wedding. After getting married, the plan was that we would move into married quarters at Northolt, and I would get used to life as an RAF wife in a leisurely fashion. But no – life is never that simple in the military.

He told me that he had been put forward for an ADC job (Aide de Camp, personal assistant) at AFCENT, the huge HQ in Holland. The boss had said that he wanted a married ADC, so that was convenient. So, only six weeks after the big day, I was whisked away to The Netherlands.

It was a very steep learning curve. I'd actually only ever been to a couple of Summer Balls, and maybe a Christmas Draw, so I had absolutely no idea how such things worked in the RAF, let alone when married to a newly appointed ADC. First of all, as the ADC's wife, you go to every formal function on your own, as he always accompanies the boss. When the boss has official visitors you are obliged to entertain the more junior members of the entourage who accompany them, and hubby may or may not be there to help. You have a lot to learn.

The next most challenging test was the monthly wives' afternoon tea party. On each occasion this would be hosted by a different nationality. When it came to Britain's turn, what else could possibly be served but Victoria sponge cakes? Those more recent arrivals, of which I was one, were invited to make a cake before the event, to be tried and tested by the more experienced senior officers' wives. The dreaded moment came, mine was duly tasted and the verdict pronounced.

'My dear, you will make an awfully good pourer.' I took that to be a rejection.

LONE BIRTHDAY GIRL

I had been married less than a month. After the honeymoon I found myself alone in a Cypriot village while my new husband had been sent away on a two-week squadron detachment. I was almost 23 and had, before my marriage, been an independent working girl. However, I had little experience of foreign countries, let alone living in one and as for military life – that was also pretty foreign to me.

In those days we had neither a telephone nor a television set and my only company in our new home was the radio, which offered me the BBC World Service or the British Forces Broadcasting Service (BFBS). I had learned that all the mail arrived through the British Forces Post Office (BFPO) and we, in Cyprus, were BFPO 53. I knew all about that from a radio programme in the 1950s called Forces Favourites which was hosted by Jean Metcalfe. Listening to the show as a teenager it had all sounded so romantic, with husbands and wives, young men and their girlfriends exchanging messages of love over the airwaves, sent to and from BFPO numbers.

So here I was approaching my birthday without my nearest and dearest, and determined to be very grown up and to make the best of it. He had bought us a new little car, a red one, which would serve very well for me especially as a newly qualified driver. He had been eager to show me around our part of the island and so I had become used to the journey through the orange plantations to the airbase at Akrotiri. This, I knew, would be where my birthday cards and (hopefully packages) would arrive.

On my special day I took a deep breath and, with passport in hand, set off in our little red 'roller-skate' towards Limassol and the main road to Akrotiri, a journey of about 20 miles. I was pleased with myself for finding the guardroom without once getting lost en route. Locating the Officers' Mess was a different matter. There were two, and I had no idea which one received all the post. As the signpost for No 1 Officers' Mess appeared first, I drove straight into its car park. Then I boldly strode through the entrance, a particularly pretty one, covered in bougainvillea. Once inside the hall I simply followed my nose until I found the wooden racks full of mail. Eureka – I had struck lucky first time. There was a stack of envelopes with my name on. I collected them up and made my way back to the car, feeling very pleased with myself.

It was some ten days later that the detachment was due back. I had received a message to say that my husband's crew were due to land at a particular time and that he would have a lift back to our home. But, on the day, they were late and I became more and more anxious. Eventually I heard a vehicle draw up outside, then my husband's voice thanking somebody for his lift. How thrilling it was that he was back home safely, and how pleased he would be to hear how well I had coped by myself.

He didn't tell me straight away. He broke it gently. Apparently, he had been delayed coming home by a summons to see his squadron commander – to be carpeted. Someone had evidently seen me picking up mail from the mess, and I must understand that wives were not allowed that privilege. I later discovered that there were even separate entrance doors for ladies. Thereafter, I often felt a certain uneasiness when walking into an Officers' Mess unescorted.

WASHDAY

We didn't have much money in those days and, being under the age of 25, lived in a small house off the base in Singapore. We certainly couldn't afford to buy so-called luxury food and had to make do with cheap ingredients like prawns. One had to be resourceful.

We had no washing machine, never mind an 'amah' to help with the housework. I took to using an old zinc bath for boiling water on the top of the kitchen stove to wash all the smaller items of clothing. For larger items I would half fill the bath with soapy water, get in and jump up and down. This form of agitating the

'Washing machine packed in again then?'

laundry worked really well and I would repeat the process with rinsing water.

Eventually, life looked up as time passed and I managed to get a job. Suddenly we could forgo the prawns and vary our diet with other exotic things and I could even afford my own 'amah'!

STRANGE COMINGS AND GOINGS

We started married life in the 1960s at RAF Gutersloh where married quarters and hirings were like gold dust. Although we qualified for housing, none was to be had, and so we were forced to find alternative accommodation. After much searching we took over a German-owned house that had once been the home of the Miele family, of washing machine fame.

The Cold War was the focal point for RAF operations at this time, and the Lightning squadrons in Germany took turns to stand 'Battle Flight' (five minutes' readiness to fly alert). As a result we often hosted members of 92 Squadron, based some distance away at RAF Geilenkirchen, sometimes with their wives. We had a German neighbour across the main road from us, who we soon realised was housebound and, with little else to do, a great net curtain twitcher. I think we gave him much to contemplate since we both worked, my husband often at night, and thus we came and went at different times – as did our mainly male guests. Imagine what our German friend must have made of his English neighbours!

HONEYMOON TACEVAL

Taceval, for anyone in the RAF from the 1960s onwards, was the be-all and end-all of life's very existence. It stood for Tactical Evaluation, and it occurred each year on every NATO Air Force station across all the NATO nations when a team of about 100 personnel from the other air force stations would descend on a base without warning and assess the operational efficiency of that base. The careers of Station Commanders and Squadron Commanders could be affected by the success, or otherwise, of their performance in their Taceval. It was seriously important.

However, there was a parallel activity on the social front which also became known as Taceval. It would occur with the same instantaneous no-notice warning, was normally led by a bunch of bachelors, and required the same instant reaction as its more serious namesake.

My introduction to this as yet unknown phenomenon happened shortly after we got married. Our wedding was on the Saturday, we grabbed a brief honeymoon night in the hotel at Scotch Corner on the A1, caught the ferry the next day to Germany, slept overnight on the ferry and arrived in our flat in Gutersloh late on the Monday afternoon. About 10 o'clock that night the doorbell rang and, when I opened the door, I was greeted by six of the squadron bachelors. Not wishing to seem inhospitable I invited them in and offered them tea or coffee. This offer was greeted with absolute silence. Luckily my husband suddenly appeared at the door with champagne bottle in hand and glasses at the ready.

Unknown to me we had been 'Tacevalled'. Whenever anyone turned up at your door and shouted 'Taceval', your success or otherwise was judged by the time it took you to have an alcoholic drink in everyone's hand. My husband clearly understood the procedure so we passed with flying colours.

I learnt very quickly, as did the other wives, that one or more bachelors approaching your house at any time of the day or night meant only one thing, so best get the beer ready. Having learnt the trick we had many successful Tacevals thereafter.

2

Five Star Living

TROUBLE IN THE COAL CELLAR

While living in married quarters at an RAF base in Germany in 1975, I had a rather unfortunate incident in the coal cellar. Our houses were heated with coke boilers in the basement that had to be kept stoked regularly 24 hours a day – a job that fell, of course, to the wives while their husbands were away on onerous detachments.

Coke was delivered by a German contractor once a month via a trap door over the coke store. It was essential that this hatch was unlocked, from the inside, before the contractor came. Otherwise, no coke would be delivered and the house could be cold for the following month! To open the trap door it was necessary to climb up onto the remaining coke and slide back a bolt. It was then also imperative to replace the retaining boards to prevent the new delivery scattering itself all over the cellar floor.

Alas, on this particular occasion I had forgotten all about the delivery until I saw the German lorry arrive and a workman start to hoist a sack of coke onto his shoulders. I raced down to the basement, frantically removed the boards, scrambled over the coke (in my best shoes) and had just opened the hatch in time for the workman to empty the first sack of coke – all over me. My German was very limited. '*Nein, nein!*' I shouted, but to no avail. My calls must have been lost in the noise as a second workman poured the next sack over me. I eventually managed to extricate myself from this deluge of coke, but by then it was all

over the floor, as replacing the boards had been the least of my worries.

Coughing and spluttering, I then had the job of trying to pile up the fuel again where it belonged. I looked like a chimney sweep. I eventually took myself to the bathroom, leaving a trail of black footprints behind me (just another bit of housework) – and tried to avoid thinking of my husband probably just downing his second beer in the comfort of the bar in Sardinia!

THE YOUNGEST FAMILIES' OFFICER

The winter of 1981 saw me posted from my first tour in Cardiff to RAF Digby in Lincolnshire. In fact this counted as a co-location, as my husband was newly stationed at RAF Binbrook, where he had been allocated an officer's married quarter (OMQ) from which I could commute daily.

Before leaving Cardiff for Binbrook I took a couple of days leave to prepare to hand my OMQ back to the army, who ran this particular patch. This process was known as Marching Out and was done under the eagle eye of the Army Barrack Warden. After a thorough inspection he declared the quarter to be immaculate and ready for the next occupant. Basking in his praise I looked forward to a reciprocal arrangement at Binbrook.

Five weary hours later I drove up to my Binbrook OMQ to be met by wind and rain but no Families' Officer. Somewhat later the situation improved with the arrival of a Mini containing what appeared to be a 15-year-old pilot officer. Ignoring me, he hot-footed it to my OMQ and disappeared inside. I resisted the temptation to ask how I, a flight lieutenant, could drive from Cardiff and be on time when it appeared that he, a more junior officer, could not do the same from Station Headquarters, and we introduced ourselves. At this point it dawned on me that my new home appeared to be in kit form, as everything was wrapped in plastic. Moreover, everywhere I looked the carpets were decked with muddy footprints. Worse, dead flies and some spiders occupied every flat surface.

This junior officer, a single man and likely to stay that way if I had anything to do with it, was unmoved by my growing distress. Foolishly he missed the point at which my distress turned to vengeance. This occurred just after I reminded him that earlier that day I had left an immaculate quarter and expected to move into something similar. At this he explained that his staff had done their best, and that as far as he was concerned I could take or leave the quarter. As an administrative officer myself I knew the book rather better than did he – a point I made while metaphorically (but only just) pinning him to the wall.

In the end he agreed to part with some money for a cleaner and left muttering darkly about my unreasonable behaviour. Little did he know how 'unreasonable' a tired WRAF officer could be!

THE FIRST MARCH OUT

We were leaving our first quarter, the 'March Out' was imminent and I was very nervous. The Families Officer had a fearsome reputation for being an absolute stickler who would leave no stone unturned. Yes, I had cleaned polished and dusted every surface including the tops of doors and cupboards, the window frames had been cleaned with a toothbrush, the cooker had been disassembled and rebuilt and now, despite its great age, gleamed as brand new – what else could I do?

Wives were not allowed to attend the March Out, so I waited with bated breath and some apprehension at our next door neighbour's. Finally my husband arrived looking rather down in the dumps. We failed – complete cooker re-clean required and he thrust a letter into my hands. Trembling with rage and not managing to hold back tears of frustration I tore open the envelope and read: 'Thank you for handing over the quarter in such an immaculate state, it has been a pleasure to take it back and I congratulate you on all your hard work especially on the cooker.'

I wasn't sure whether to kill or kiss my mischievous husband. It was the only time in 30 years of service life that I ever got an official 'thank you' for a March Out – but then that Families Officer was a woman.

FULLY FURNISHED

Our posting to Scotland had been arranged for six months. We were fairly newly married and as my husband was a very junior officer we were only entitled to the smallest quarter, but it had been agreed that we could have one that was fully furnished with a large south-facing garden.

When we arrived in the environs of the station my heart sank – everywhere was surrounded by high fences and rolls of barbed wire, the houses were grey with dingy pebbledash and it was cold and dreary. The removal van containing our few possessions (mainly wedding presents) followed us to our allotted house which, although the same dismal grey, did have the promised potential garden. My husband met the Families Officer to begin the 'March In' – wives were not allowed to be present.

There was a problem: no furniture – apparently this house was on an MOD list of 'de-furnished' quarters and, despite the fact that there was plenty of furniture in stores, it could on no account be put into this house. So began a stately procession, including the removal van, round the married patch to find another quarter with furniture. The first one offered had serious problems, fully kitted out but the lounge ceiling had fallen in; the second had no garden to speak of; the third was a higher grade and we simply could not afford the rent. So, after the convoy completed its circumnavigation, we decided to accept the first quarter without furniture.

The removal men were highly amused as we left them unloading our treasures – china, cut glass, cutlery and fridge freezer – while we went out to buy a bed. Before we had even set off our next-door neighbours came to say hello and then returned bearing camping table and chairs. All evening our doorbell rang as increasingly distant neighbours came to offer spare bits of furniture which we gladly accepted.

Over the next few months we did manage to furnish our home with things from the local auction house. We were still on a very tight budget so everything came back on the top of our car, on the way to our garden for de-woodworming, most of it in need of serious 'tlc' if not complete reupholstering. Our arrival and subsequent home-building provided hours of amusement for both our new friends and us.

A NEW KITCHEN

Sometime back in the 1970s we took over a quarter at a well-known HQ in NW Germany. The adjacent quarters had all recently had a kitchen make-over, courtesy of MPBW (Ministry of Public Buildings and Works). On enquiring with the Families Office why our particular quarter had been missed, we were advised that the previous occupants had declined the offer for their kitchen to be renovated because they were soon to be posted. They were perfectly happy to stick with the old one and certainly didn't want the upheaval of major works in the house just as they were about to move. What's more, the work-team had already moved on and there was no possibility of them returning just to modernise OUR kitchen.

At this point we felt we should write to the Families Officer to point out the unfairness of the situation, not expecting a quick response:

Dear Families Officer,

As you are probably aware the kitchen at our quarter was omitted from the modernisation programme because the previous occupants declined it.

Since moving into the quarter I have found the kitchen to be very inconvenient and old-fashioned. A particular concern is that the draining board leading to the sink has an unusual slant which causes excess water to drain on to the floor, instead of into the basin. This has resulted in my developing webbed feet and having to wear Wellington boots to wash-up.

Against this background I hope you will give consideration to changing your earlier decision.

Yours sincerely, …

This letter was submitted to the Families Office on a Friday afternoon. On Monday morning MPBW were at the door to take a look and, a week later, I had a beautiful renovated kitchen!

28

'Hurry up love. I need 'em!'

THE MILKMAN

My memories of RAF Waddington in the 1970s, when we lived there with three Vulcan squadrons, provoke the sound of a wailing siren during the night signalling the start of a dispersal exercise. Those rude awakenings saw our menfolk struggling into flying suits, grabbing holdalls and 'nav' bags and, eventually, roaring off into the night sky. After he had slammed the front door I would drift back to sleep with one ear tuned, waiting for the sound of the departing jets. On a cold still night one would think that the entire V Force had taken off.

These rapid deployments to secret, classified locations were difficult to cope with. You never knew how far they went or for how long they'd be gone. Inevitably there would be some domestic crisis looming – a sick child, the 'twin tub' breaking down, or our elderly car refusing to start during a freezing and foggy Lincoln-shire morning.

As my husband vanished into the night on one occasion I was particularly anxious, as we had planned our son's christening for the following week and many family members would be travelling to Lincoln for the service in the RAF chapel of the cathedral. We families had no idea when to expect our husbands' return. I must have appeared really down in the dumps when the milkman called with his weekly bill.

'Don't worry luv,' he said. 'They're only gone 'til Friday.'

'What? Have you got a crystal ball or something?'

'Your ole man's on 50 Squadron isn't he? Well they left a note for me to deliver the usual on Friday.'

This was a revelation to me – and became a bit of a joke around the station. Sadly, however, our milkman was never able to feed his lonely customers such 'inside information' again!

FRIENDLY AIR MARSHALS

Having VIPs to stay is always fraught with possible dangers but one such visit was particularly daunting. It all centred on a significant squadron reunion when we found ourselves (my husband as CO) offering accommodation to not one, but two air marshals, one wife and one young son.

Having four bedrooms on the first floor but only one bathroom (well this was 1991), my husband and I vacated our room for one senior officer, leaving the other and his wife further down the corridor (opposite the bathroom/loo) with their young son next door to them and us at the end. At some time during the night, after answering a call of nature, one senior officer became

disorientated and started to get into bed with our second visitor and his wife. This couple, assuming that the midnight prowler was their son, gave him short shrift, demanding that he return to his own room immediately. This roused our wanderer sufficiently for him to realise his mistake and for the couple to recognise the intruder for who he truly was.

There was more than one red male face at breakfast the next morning, several polite apologies and much hilarity amongst the ladies!

THE AFTERNOON NAP

It was the day after the summer ball at RAF Cranwell. My next-door neighbour had had a very enjoyable night but was suffering from a rather heavy hangover. By the afternoon she decided to retire to her bed for a gentle snooze. Her two little girls were home from school and so she explained that Mummy was going to have a little lie down and was not to be disturbed by anyone. It was an extremely hot afternoon so she crashed out naked on her bed, with the window slightly ajar and the curtains open to allow a breeze.

On waking, feeling a million times better, she eventually dressed and went downstairs to face the world. A note lay on the mat below the letterbox together with a bill for £5. It read: 'Dear Mrs Smith, as arranged on my last visit, all windows cleaned upstairs and down. Will collect money on next visit.'

TREETOPS

'Treetops' was a group of huts at RAF Leuchars in Scotland which had been used during World War II for storage. During the 1960s there was a shortage of Officer Married Quarters at Leuchars and the huts had been hastily reconfigured as sub-standard married accommodation for the under 25s. I was newly married and one of these huts became our first home. There was a real community spirit on this little married patch as we shared the pitfalls of living in huts that were freezing cold, had suspect plumbing, and were prime targets for Tacevals and instant parties.

Years later we returned to RAF Leuchars where my husband was the Station Commander. On his first inspection of the station he suddenly asked the driver to halt the car at an unscheduled stop. The confused Station Warrant Officer who was also in the car asked my husband why he wanted to see this particular building. My husband replied that he used to live here. There was amazement on the Warrant Officer's face because our first family home was now being used as the Scout Hut.

SUB-STANDARD ACCOMMODATION

My husband was posted to RAF Leuchars in Scotland in January 1971. We were entitled to a type 5 married quarter, the smallest type, but unfortunately none was available and we were obliged to take a house in 'Treetops'.

During the 'March In' and inventory check, the housing officer explained that our new home used to be an electronics store in the early days of the station. I discovered there were many interesting nooks and crannies and lots of cupboard space designed to store essential electrical items of that bygone era. All this storage space would, in fact, come to be most useful for our household goods and personal things.

Once settled, I made a visit to my neighbour. Her house, I noticed, had a ramp leading up to double front doors – this was not a normal frontage of an officer's quarter. Once inside, I couldn't help but comment upon the beautifully tiled white walls.

'Oh, this used to be the station mortuary during the Second World War!' she explained.

BLOCKED DRAINS

'So! The Sgt's Mess had a curry last night!'

It was a normal Saturday morning in our quarter at Treetops. Except that on this particular day there seemed to be dreadful whiff coming from the front door. Opening it up, I saw what I can only describe as effluent waste flowing down the road.

Horror of horrors! I immediately phoned the duty housing engineer. He duly came along and said that he would investigate the source of this unpleasant trail straight away. His idea was to put a bright orange dye into the 'upstream' drains and wait for nature to take its course. It wasn't long before the orange-tainted offending waste reached the front of our quarter. I called the engineer again, who promptly came to inspect and draw his conclusions.

'Well, where is the source?' I asked him.

'I'm afraid that it's coming from a fracture in a sewer in the Sergeants' Mess,' he told me.

When I recounted the result of the engineer's experiment to my husband, he quipped, 'Now we know what was on the menu last night.'

THE COLDEST QUARTER

The moment I crossed the threshold, I knew that this was going to be a very cold house on the RAF Cranwell patch. The Marching In Officer admitted that it had been unoccupied for a while, but thought that we were lucky to be offered this four-bedroom quarter for the short six-month Air Warfare Course. Now that he had fired up the boiler, he assured me, it would soon warm up.

It never warmed up! No amount of cling film or polythene would block out the bitterly cold winds that swept across Lincolnshire that winter. My husband and I set up our refuge in the smallest bedroom and lived mostly in the kitchen.

We were close to cancelling our first supper party when the boiler failed to pass any life-blood to the radiators, and my husband had to refit the plug on an ugly old electric fire that had been consigned to the garage. Our gallant guests, who had been warned in advance of our ice-box conditions, duly arrived imaginatively dressed in ski suits, hats and mittens!

It happened that our neighbour was a Canadian attending the same course as my husband. (An ex-monk, he had by some divine intervention given up his holy orders to become a fighter pilot – but that's another story!) In spite of thinking that this was nothing like as severe as a Canadian winter, his wife took pity on me. It seemed that their house was considerably warmer than ours – hot actually, as the Canadian government was paying their fuel bills. She would frequently kick at my back door during the late morning and, with a gin and tonic in each hand, ask which pub we should go to for our nourishing lunch.

Towards the end of our six-month stay I was preparing the quarter for Marching Out. As I was paying the window cleaner, I was still grumbling about the cold.

'Well luv, ye'know, this house never got insulated like the rest – in fact, it's not often occupied!'

HOUSE STAFF

In the late 1980s we moved to RAF Lyneham into a somewhat old-fashioned married quarter. During our first evening, settling in, the doorbell rang. I went to the front door – no one there. I went to the back door – no one there. A mystery. It rang a third time – no one at either door.

Then a shout from the bathroom – husband calling.

'I thought that pressing this button by the bath might get me a G&T – doesn't seem to be working too well!'

I'll leave you to guess my reply.

TOILET SEAT

Our two-year-old boy had discovered the fun of dropping his toys and other items into the lavatory bowl. I spoke to the housing officer about the problem because I was worried that one of the larger items might get trapped in the U bend and block the toilet. I requested that a cover or standard lid be fitted to the toilet. The housing officer was sympathetic to my cry for help but asked, 'What rank is your husband?'

'He's a flight lieutenant,' I replied.

'I'm sorry, Ma'am, but I'm unable to help you. Your husband is not entitled to a cover, as he has to be at least a wing commander.'

'Ah! I see Jim's been promoted!'

MOVING TO GERMANY

We were posted to Germany for my husband to do a flying tour on Phantoms, starting two weeks before Christmas. We cleaned our quarter in Lincolnshire to within an inch of its life, which included scrubbing all parts of the toilet with a toothbrush and cleaning the cooker with a Black and Decker wire brush attachment. March Out completed, we discovered there were no quarters available at our new station, Bruggen. Not to be foiled we decided that, although I was six months pregnant, I would travel out with my husband and find somewhere to live when we got there.

Arriving late in the day at the RAF Bruggen Officers' Mess, Hubby was allocated a room on the ground floor. We both managed to sleep in his single-bedded room overnight but the next morning we parted company as he reported to his new squadron for work. I had to climb out of his bedroom window (no wives allowed) and go off to find somewhere to live.

I visited a few places and then found a wooden chalet in a nearby forest. After completing the rental contract, we moved in and unpacked our belongings for the next few months. Within four days we were informed there was now a flat in quarters that we could move into. If, however, we turned it down we would not be eligible again until everyone else on the waiting list had been found a quarter. So, we cleaned the chalet to within an inch of its life and went across to our new flat. It was only then that we found out it was new, as in just built, complete with builders' trash and dust everywhere. So we cleaned the flat to within an inch of its life and moved into our new home.

By this time it was a few days before Christmas. We travelled home to the Midlands. The following day I thought I had a stomach upset. Having tried 'kaolin' and everything else I could think of, my mother tentatively suggested that maybe I was having the baby.

The ambulance arrived in double quick time and I was taken into hospital where it was confirmed – my mother was right. They did a blood test and informed me that I was dehydrated, exhausted and starving. What had I been doing, they exclaimed!

Well, in the last two weeks I had moved house three times, cleaned three houses to within an inch of their lives, and travelled backwards and forwards across the continent. You can imagine their reply.

THE YELLOW SUBMARINE

Station Commanders' houses are usually quite special, spacious with five or six bedrooms often on three floors, elegant in parts, have large gardens and impressive frontage and a prime position on the married patch. Ours definitely did not fit this bill!

We arrived in pouring rain, and it continued to rain for 40+ days after our arrival. It was difficult to locate the house; it appeared to be in some sort of derelict building site or partly demolished airfield. There was no definite married patch, just a square of houses behind a sodden sports field. The outside was unimpressive and the house smaller than the one we had just left, but the inside was more than a bit of a disappointment. The lounge was long, thin and drab, the kitchen old-fashioned with a strange wall separating an area later identified as the 'ironing area' for the staff, the four bedrooms and avocado bathroom outdated and shabby; but the downstairs cloakroom provided the biggest shock and had to be seen to be believed.

It was yellow. The toilet was yellow, the wash basin was yellow and set in garish yellow-tiled work surface which continued halfway up one wall on which hung a huge mirror. This reflected the 60s wallpaper: yellow, pink, orange and purple flowers about a foot in diameter. The curtains were yellow and the floor was red quarry tiles. Oh dear! We had entered a time warp and what were our visiting VIPs going to think when they had to use the facilities? It was certainly not a place to go if you were feeling at all queasy or had over-indulged in a too-delicious dinner and generous hospitality.

This room became the priority for change, and after much debate and argument it was reluctantly agreed by the Estates Office to mute its revolting colour scheme by painting the walls and tiles magnolia (a favourite RAF Married Quarter colour) and providing a neutral carpet. The yellow toilet and washbasin survived to remind us of the room that was dubbed 'The Yellow Submarine'.

We did have some wonderful times in that house, we entertained amazing people and it was a privilege to live there, but the house itself never quite lived up to its role as 'The Station Commander's House'.

SHUFFLING BEDS

In the week before Christmas we moved to RAF Leeming, but decided not to unpack as we were spending the holiday with family in Scotland. A very kind couple who lived on the opposite side of the square, whom we hardly knew, welcomed us onto the base with a lovely supper. They were expecting lots of visitors over the festive season so we offered them our quarter as extra sleeping accommodation.

We travelled north the next morning but disaster stuck when we called into the Metro Centre in Newcastle. Our car, complete with all our luggage, golf clubs, shooting gear, dinner dress, wellingtons, children's clothes, games and Christmas presents, was stolen from the car park. The police were informed and were very sympathetic – the bobby on duty described my husband as 'Mr Respectable' when the matter of the missing firearm was reported to his senior.

What were we to do? We were carless, the children possessed only the clothes they stood up in, none of us now owned a toothbrush, and we were an hour away from our latest home.

The only people we knew on the base were our previous night's hosts so we called them. They sounded shocked and breathless to hear from us but kindly agreed to come and collect us. There would be a bit of a delay though.

On the way back to Leeming we learnt two things. First, the car had been found, all contents had been removed but it was completely burnt out. Second, our kind rescuers had been delayed because, when we rang, they were in the process of moving our double bed into their quarter; it was already halfway down the road but they felt obliged to put it back before they collected us.

We had a second night of great hospitality and thoroughly drowned our sorrows before departing to our respective beds. The next day we drove north in our second car, a very beaten-up old Metro, and our neighbours moved our bed once again, this time in our full knowledge and with our complete blessing.

A TEMPORARY RESIDENCE

Back in 1974 things happened so quickly that, six months later, I couldn't remember the date of birth of my new baby.

We had bought our first house in Shropshire and moved in and moved out in the space of three months, which happened to be the last three months of my pregnancy. This was due to the sudden and unexpected notice of my husband's posting to HQ RAF Germany as an ADC (personal assistant). Just one week later he was obliged to report for duty, leaving me to tie up the loose ends and prepare the house for letting – and give birth in regulation time. He would find us a quarter then return in two weeks to drive the baby, our 2-year-old son and me out to Rheindahlen. Somehow I managed to meet the deadline, he flew back to UK, we packed up the car and left the house we were never to live in again.

He broke the news en route. A quarter was not yet available and therefore we would have to make do for a while in Cassells House which, he explained, was a 'transit hostel'. However, it wasn't all bad news. Since he had survived the first two weeks in his new job, his boss, the Air Marshal, declared that he and his wife needed a break and therefore my beloved could do likewise and spend time with me and his expanded family.

It was with some trepidation that we neared our destination after the long trip. It was already dark and the baby was ready for feeding again. We were tired and our 2-year-old was definitely at the end of his tether. We passed the signs to JHQ and turned off onto a wooded drive that opened out in front of a large and imposing house.

'We're here!' my husband shouted triumphantly. My spirits lifted, this didn't look like any old hostel. As we drew up to the entrance a uniformed steward stepped out and opened the car door.

'Welcome to Germany.'

I looked at my husband, bemused.

This was not Cassells House, he explained but the Air Marshal's residence. He and his wife had insisted we stay there while they were on leave.

For one luxurious week we were looked after, spoilt and cosseted by the house staff! The only setback during that memorable time was when our inquisitive little boy found the only 'toy' in the house – a scale model of a 'John Player Special' racing car which he knocked from its pride of place to shatter on a tiled floor. My poor beloved spent many of his evenings painstakingly repairing the model, which the Air Marshal had meticulously and proudly constructed! Happily, the excess glue went unnoticed, certainly through to the end of our tour.

3

The Little Darlings

TO PEE OR NOT TO PEE

The family had just moved with the Harrier force to Gutersloh in Germany. My youngest daughter, all of 2 and walking, used to follow a group of young 5-year-old boys round the corner to an old air-raid shelter. Here she would watch with obvious fascination as they showed off their prowess as to how far they could pee.

Not long after we had settled, the Station Chaplain called by at about tea time. As we were chatting on the front door step our daughter decided to join in, but she was completely naked and holding a plastic cup. She waited until she had the Padre's full attention then, standing, she opened her legs and peed into the cup on the ground.

I shrieked with laughter as the Padre rushed off, never to call again, probably preferring the company of junior fighter pilots. Clearly the Padre's training at Theological College never covered such realities of family life!

ARMY TRAINING

My second posting as the wife of an RAF officer was very convenient. It was only our fourth move! I was very excited. He said that we would do at least two tours at Brize Norton, plus the training. My goodness, that would mean at least six years. All went well, we sold one house and bought another in the perfect place only about 20 minutes' drive from Brize, and I was pregnant as well – excellent.

One week after moving in he came home from work and said, 'We are posted, well not immediately as I have to finish the course. So, we don't have to actually move for another six months.'

The next thing to do was to have the baby. In those days the large hospital in Oxford had special facilities for expectant military wives but, having visited, I decided not to have my baby there as instead of my name at the end of the bed, it would have been 'Wife of …' or even worse, W/O.

All went well at our local cottage hospital and my baby was born. He had his first move at 6 weeks, his second at 8 months and his third at 9½ months. Very good training and perhaps no wonder that he went on to join the army.

MY LITTLE BROTHER

Back in the 1950s overseas travel was very expensive, and children coming home from boarding school to see their parents often had to travel on their own. Usually they were taken to the airport, handed over to BOAC air stewardesses who made sure that they got onto the correct aircraft, and were then met at the destination airport by their doting parents.

My parents were living at RAF Bruggen, a station in Germany close to the Dutch border. The currency in those days was the Deutschmark for which, in 1955, the exchange rate was eight to £1. My brother, aged 8½ years, was due to return to his prep school in Shrewsbury. Our parents could not afford the air flight so he was to go back by train from Moenchengladbach to the Hook of Holland and then by ferry to Harwich. Unfortunately our parents got caught in the rush-hour traffic and arrived at Moenchengladbach train station just minutes before the train was due to depart. They rushed across the platform and found a compartment with a spare seat.

His compartment was quite full of people who watched in fascination as this little chap was bundled onto the train. They then looked slightly boggle-eyed as his mother asked them to keep an eye on him to the Hook of Holland, where he had to get off. My brother was neatly dressed in his school blazer, shorts and cap. Mother popped his passport in one pocket and tickets in the other, together with a little money for emergencies, and waved a tearful farewell as the guard blew his whistle and the train pulled out.

To be fair, my mother was slightly dazed and wondered what on earth she had just done – and then worried the rest of the day and night about it. My brother, on the other hand, just took it all in his stride and thought this was the greatest adventure ever. When he reached the Hook of Holland he asked which boat went to

England, receiving some incredulous questions in return, such as, 'Are you actually on your own?'

He found the ferry and his cabin, which had two double bunks and a bathroom down the corridor. He remembers wandering around the boat, having a small snack and then deciding it was time for bed. Later that night he woke up to hear someone in another bunk snoring. He was slightly nervous, but as he did not want to say anything he went back to sleep and eventually woke up to the sound of the boat docking in Harwich.

Yes, he made it to his school whereupon a call was booked to very relieved parents. A child travelling alone in those days was not, in fact, that unusual – a friend of mine, whose son had to take a similar route, had stuck his name in his top pocket, just in case he forgot it!

It was quite tough for families back then; children who went to boarding school had just one paid ticket a year for the holidays. One year we didn't see my brother at all. Overseas telephone calls had to be booked in advance and were prohibitively expensive. Most overseas communication was by post.

My mother's journal for that day reads simply, 'He looked very smart in his school uniform. Very worried.'

A FLAMING GOOD PARTY

I don't know about you, but for me children's birthdays come under the title of 'confined hell'. In fact giving a dinner party is infinitely preferable. However, we want to please our little darlings and it is, for them, a day of great celebration. As mummies, we aim to please.

This particular birthday party had a particular edge; my daughter and her greatest friend in her class decided to celebrate together. Marvellous. It meant the whole class could be invited and we would gather in the Officers' Mess. Even better, we would have a children's entertainer, a very novel idea in those days.

'*Birthday* cake? Nah, issa volcano!'

Everything had been going swimmingly; the children were thoroughly enjoying themselves, rushing around the spacious rooms of the Mess. Then they all sat down to birthday tea. I had made the most superb birthday cake. It was a fairy castle, just like the one in Disney World. Very tall turrets complete with doilies on top and meringue blobs to hold them in place added a distinctly fairy-like touch.

The candles were lit and, as we started to sing 'Happy Birthday', the paper doilies caught fire! Quick as a flash I attempted to douse the flames with my hands, but the fire was getting rather fierce. By this time the children were diving for cover under the table, the few parents present were completely mesmerised, and the Mess Manager, bless him, was looking somewhat concerned, the room having only just been redecorated.

Well, of course, we soon had everything under control, even if the cake was a little charred. I never really understood why none of the children wanted to even try it. One father, collecting his son, asked if he had enjoyed the party. The boy replied, 'It was fantastic, Dad! The cake exploded!'

BEHIND CLOSED DOORS

It was way back in the 1960s and our first tour in Cyprus. My husband was flying Canberras in those days, and looking through his log book has reminded me of the many and frequent occasions he was away on detachment in Malta, Teheran and Sharjah, as well as the UK.

It was always great excitement for the children to see their beloved daddy come home and he would always bring back all sorts of presents for them and for me. Some chosen ones, like precious stone pendants, copper jugs, trays and chafing dishes, might be hidden to be given on special occasions.

After one such home-coming, while the children were at school, my husband and I were in our bedroom with the door firmly locked. Suddenly there was the rattling of the door handle and a small voice calling, 'I want to come in.'

My husband and I looked at each other, then that small voice yelled, 'I know what you're doing!'

We called back, 'And what do you think we are doing?'

'You're looking at my Christmas presents!' he shouted.

RED WELLIES

Blind panic! It is 7.00 am; my 2-year-old is missing and is nowhere to be found. We are living in married quarters in amongst civilian

'But it *isn't* dress down day!'

houses on a busy road in Stanmore, north London. His father left for work at 6.00 am when I heard the gate clang shut.

Just as I was about to extend my search the doorbell rang. There was my son, stark naked except for a pair of red wellies, in the arms of a large burly ambulance man. He had been found at the end of the road, about half a mile from home, on his way to the Tube station, following his father's route to work. No one in the civilian houses along the street knew who he was, so they suggested trying the RAF homes. The affluent local community always seemed to think that we lowered the tone of the area and, on that occasion, I feel they had reason.

THE SCHOOL SATCHEL

In 1982 we were living in married quarters – behind the wire – at RAF Kinloss. My husband was engaged in the Falklands War and was away from home based on Ascension Island. Our young son, then aged 8, attended Kinloss Primary School. As such, he was usually able to walk home with his friends at the end of the day via the rear school gate, which opened directly onto the base. (I normally walked with him in the morning to make sure he got to school on time!) The route from school took him past the two station churches, which were opposite the Sergeants' Mess, across a road, then past the Officers' Mess to the married quarters patch.

One afternoon he returned home as usual, changed out of his school uniform, had a snack and disappeared out to play with his friends. A few minutes later, I heard a voice booming through a loud-hailer. The voice persisted with varied volume and was obviously being delivered from a vehicle that was travelling around married quarters. I went outside to listen more carefully. The message via the loud-hailer came over loud and clear. 'A suspect object resembling a child's school satchel has been seen on the ground opposite the Sergeants' Mess and will be blown up if unclaimed.'

I immediately went indoors to check that my son had hung his satchel in its usual place in the cloakroom. It wasn't there! I began to go 'hot and cold', then decided that he must have taken it up to his bedroom and hurried upstairs to look. No satchel there either! Now I really was beginning to panic and dashed outside to see if I could find my son. Luckily he was heading home, wondering what the noise was all about. I asked him about his satchel and he looked blankly at me.

'It's not on the usual hook or in your bedroom,' I said. 'Did you put it down somewhere on the way home from school?'

'Well,' he replied, 'I did stop to climb a tree by the church.'

'That's it!' I exclaimed. The church was opposite the Sergeants' Mess.

Next moment I was on the phone and, before I knew it, an official car with Wing Commander Ops and his sergeant drew up outside the house. My son and I got in and were driven close to the scene of the incident. I was mortified to learn that the road past the two churches had been closed and the Sergeants' Mess evacuated. My son was taken forward a few steps and the offending satchel pointed out to him. 'Yes, that's mine,' he acknowledged.

How I wished the ground would just open and swallow me up. To think that my child had almost caused the station to come to a grinding halt! However, if any good came of the incident, apart from being a topic of amusement to many, it was that my son did become more responsible for his possessions – for a while at least!

THE POTTY

We all know that travelling with two small children can be very difficult. However, on this occasion I was very excited because we were on our way to Canada on an exchange posting with the Canadian Air Force. Our son was barely 16 months old and our daughter, aged only 4 weeks, was just old enough to be allowed to fly in an RAF aircraft. Our posting instruction had indicated that we could expect to be living in hotels for several weeks at least, first in Ottawa then moving on to Bagotville in Quebec. Once there, it would be up to us to find a house to rent for six months before moving on yet again to Chatham in New Brunswick. With all this moving about, our array of bags, boxes and suitcases was impressive.

The flight out from Brize Norton in the RAF Comet went as well as could be expected, and I had to be well organised. It was in the days long before disposable nappies, instant baby foods or electronic games, so I was armed with all the usual paraphernalia including teddy bears, nappies, change of clothes, toys and a potty – all distributed between several bags. I had already started potty

R.ENRUT

training my 16-month-old because I decided that washing out two lots of nappies in a hotel room was not an option.

The flight was actually quite exciting because I was the only female on board, and with two small children we were separated from the other forces passengers in our own area with plenty of space to accommodate us plus all the extra hand luggage. However, the flight did land later than planned and we only had 10 minutes to cross the airport to the other terminal for our onward flight.

Luckily the stewards realised our predicament and ensured that we were first off the aircraft. It soon became obvious that, with each of us carrying a child, we could not manage all the luggage and be able to run.

Fortunately help was at hand and some kind gentleman appeared from nowhere and said, 'Give me a bag and don't worry.' Together we made the ten-minute dash and arrived breathless at the gate. As I turned round to thank my unknown hero for all his help, I found I was too late. He had disappeared, having set down the bag he had been carrying – together with the potty which he had balanced squarely on the top!

It was sometime later, as I was reading the *RAF News*, that I recognised his picture – he was a very senior RAF officer, an Air Marshal who, unknown to us, had been travelling on our aircraft. I do hope that he reads this tale and perhaps recognises himself, because I would very much like to thank him personally after all this time for his invaluable help in our hour of need. It marked the start of a very happy and memorable tour in Canada. (And my grandchildren now use that same, well-travelled potty.)

MEMORIES OF CHILDHOOD

Don't you find that memories of childhood can come shooting alive in seconds, with a sudden whiff of a scent, a distant sound, or a subtle taste? Suddenly you are back in that moment surrounded by its vision. My childhood was a canvas of amazing events, and for that I must thank my parents, who allowed me to explore on my own wherever they served in the world. But also, thank you to the RAF for giving me such a rich and varied childhood. Always on the move, six months here, one year there but maybe two or more if we were lucky. Possibly fifteen different schools. One forgets!

Arriving, by plane, in a new country for the first time gets one's nostrils sniffing. The country's complete character is immediately there, its identity; the smells and the sounds carried on a warm wind. Of course AVTUR (aviation fuel) is the basic smell from the surrounding aircraft sitting on hot tarmac, but it heralds the beginning of new excitement, new people, new things to experience and a strange culture to be explored. To a child, this is an adventure indeed!

Part of my childhood was spent in Egypt. School was just a half day, the rest of the time was spent running around half naked, in the warm Egyptian sun, listening to the Muezzin calls five times daily, making dens with friends, climbing casuarina trees and listening to the light wind blowing softly through their needles. The smell of the sand from the desert, dogs barking in the background.

Another large part of my childhood was spent in Germany where we had the whole Continent right on our door step. Do we take a left or right out of our street? Should we nip into Holland, or what about Belgium? Hmm, I think we'll make it to France for a picnic – what a choice.

There was every conceivable sporting facility in an overseas Camp, often a riding stable, swimming pool, squash and tennis courts, a golf course, and of course a school, all within the confines of the Base. Bruggen had no secondary school though, and so we would ride on a bus to Rheindahlen. I eventually had a taste of being educated at Tildonk, an Ursuline convent in Belgium. Memories of our nuns roller-skating around the playground in their habits come instantly to mind and finally, but difficult to beat, was an out-of-this-world introduction to Lindt chocolate. Now I recognise the beginning of a life-long addiction! Sometimes civilian friends would be curious as to how we could put up with such an unreal lifestyle. I found it very difficult to empathise with their views. It was, after all, my existence and the only life I knew.

Summing up, my childhood was full of excitement, full of play, full of exploring, undoubtedly helped by the security of a close-knit family. Although I took it for granted then, I owe much to the undeniable freedom one had living within the very secure environment of an RAF camp. Without doubt, I must thank the Royal Air Force for an incredibly rich and enjoyable childhood.

THE BATTLE OF BRITAIN BABY

There were four of us on the squadron all expecting babies within three months of each other. For three of us it was to be our first baby and we were always comparing notes and asking advice from the fourth, an experienced mum.

Number one baby was born and I was the next due. However, as we all know, where babies are concerned there are no exact rules. My baby was a week overdue and I was dismayed to learn that the next baby in line had now also been born. I was determined to get things moving. All the old wives' tales had been tried so I went blackberry picking, stretching and jumping to get the choicest fruits and hopefully get the baby moving. However, this was in the days of the Cold War and I had forgotten that my husband was on QRA (Quick Reaction Alert). This meant that he and another pilot would sit, eat and sleep next to their fully armed Lightning aircraft. They had to be airborne within ten minutes to intercept any Russian aircraft approaching the Iceland – Faeroes Gap several hundred miles to the north of our home in Scotland.

That night the inevitable happened, and at around midnight my waters broke and contractions started. I was excited but also very nervous. I phoned the hospital and they told me to get in as soon as possible. I did not tell them that I was home alone with no near neighbours, and that my husband and friend were defending the western world all on their own.

Without even considering an ambulance at what must now have been about one o'clock in the morning, I phoned my husband to explain what was happening and after some discussion we decided that I would drive the thirty-minute journey to pick him up and, at the same time, he would phone another pilot to come and take his place on QRA. Once he was relieved of his duties, we could then continue the journey to hospital together.

All went according to plan. We got to the hospital and the contractions were getting closer, but because it was a first baby it was probably going to take its time. And so it did. Later that morning my husband was looking longingly out of the window across the estuary to RAF Leuchars. I had forgotten it was 15th September, Battle of Britain Day, and that there was a spectacular air display in progress. He encouraged me to get out of bed between contractions and I did manage to see one of Concorde's very first flypasts. However, I soon spotted my husband in discussion with the midwife seeking reassurance that I was going to be some while yet. He would therefore have time to nip back to the squadron, see as much of the air show as possible, including the Red Arrows, and still be back in time for the birth.

As he disappeared, so did my contractions. It was as though everything just stopped and was put on hold. He eventually returned at the end of the afternoon and what had started so expectantly at midnight, resumed that evening; I eventually produced our son on Battle of Britain Day, at ten o'clock that night. I can forgive my husband for not being at home when things started; I can forgive him for making me drive myself to hospital but, to this day, I cannot forgive him for prolonging what should have been a straightforward first birth by leaving me so that he could go and watch an air show! I should have realised then what I know only too well now – that I would always be competing against his beloved Air Force.

A FATHER AND DAUGHTER CONVERSATION

My husband is certainly not known for his tolerance of other drivers on the road, especially women, unless of course they happen to be driving him home from a party. So, much to my amusement, when he became boss of a Tornado squadron he was a little taken aback to find that he would be father-figure to the Air Force's first female fast-jet navigator. Fortunately she turned out to be very good at her job, and he was eventually forced to admit that he had modified his opinion about women and their abilities.

At the same time our daughter was studying for her A levels and in the process of making career choices. She was a very gifted dancer, a county hockey player and had passed her driving test first time! So, in my husband's opinion, she was proving to be well coordinated, very talented and, all in all, a chip off the old block.

She secured a place at university to study dance and, like all good fathers, he was concerned about her future job prospects and what career path she might follow. While he was in the process of letting her know his thoughts about what options to consider, I overheard the following conversation.

'Have you ever thought of joining the Royal Air Force?' and, thinking he was paying her the greatest compliment, 'You would make a good pilot.'

There was a slight pause before she calmly replied, 'Dad, I thought you had greater aspirations for me than that!'

And that was the end of the discussion. She did not join the RAF, but gained a degree in dance, going on to work very successfully in television.

OUT OF THE MOUTHS OF BABES

Detachments form a significant part of the everyday life of a Service family – but how do the children really view them? During a period in the mid 1980s when my husband was involved in bringing a new jet into service, he was naturally away for some considerable time, coming home for weekends whenever possible.

Our 4-year-old son was apparently taking this all in his stride, until the day he hugged the uniformed knees of the visiting Station Chaplain, crying 'Daddy!' and then, 48 hours later when his father appeared, met him at the front door declaring, 'I'll show you where you sleep!'

DEFINING YOUR ROLE

As a woman married to a serviceman, your role changes as the years roll by – from newly married, childless, junior pilot's wife, to the 'small children under your feet all the time' mother, to the Squadron Commander's wife with an enormous 'family' to care for.

My role was finally decided for me by a small child who battered on our front door one day. 'Are you Misty's mum? Can she come out to play?'

'Misty' was our 4-year-old Cocker spaniel. Enough said!

EGYPTIAN COCA COLA

One of the most exciting aspects of growing up within a Service family in the 1950s was going to live in distant countries which no one in England really cared or thought about. We were allowed to take a few personal items, so that packing wasn't a big deal. Houses then were completely furnished right down to the cruet set.

It was just before the Suez Crisis and I found myself in Egypt; Ismailia to be exact. We lived in a beautiful large bungalow with a wide veranda surrounding the whole building; sometimes, for fun, my brother and I would sleep out there. Drinking water had to be boiled and then kept in a huge white fridge. It was really good to drink, unlike the watered down evaporated milk we were given at our school in Fayad.

Due to the impending Suez Crisis we were not allowed to go to many places and, indeed, we had an armed guard on our school bus. This seemed so natural to us and, although we were not allowed to go into the town of Ismailia, we were allowed to use the service sailing club at Lake Timsah each afternoon. Here we all learnt to sail and swim. I shall always remember swimming out to pontoons through shoals of baby jellyfish and acting as ballast as our fathers skippered stately 'Bordeaux' dinghies.

However, included in these idyllic afternoons was my first foray into the world of ice-cold pop drink, an almost indescribable highlight for a 9-year-old. There was ice cream soda that tasted out of this world, just like fizzy vanilla ice cream, but without the cone. However, Coca Cola, well that was a different matter – a world apart in taste. This small iconic glass bottle, the fizz at the top and the lively dark liquid below held my fascination, it was indescribably delicious. I would slowly suck this elixir through a paper straw, staving off the eventual noisy cacophony of my straw tugging at the bottom of an empty bottle. An ice-cold drink such as this was heaven on earth, and a treat beyond all dreams. To add to the impact, the advertising was wonderfully weird; billboards would catch your eye with the same red scrawl, but the spelling would be Cole Coke, Coka Cola, Coke Cole. Unwittingly good advertising I guess, because I still remember it to this day!

VIRGIN MUMMY

We had recently moved to an RAF Station in Cambridgeshire where my husband was proud to take command of his own squadron. I had a job as a teacher in a local school where our 7-year-old son was a pupil. On that particular morning in December we were doing the school run and my little chap was strapped into the back seat as usual. Out of the blue he unexpectedly asked, 'Are you a virgin Mummy?'

Like most parents confronted by a difficult question, concentrating on the traffic and negotiating a busy intersection, I calmly responded, 'Just wait a moment, sweetheart.'

He was dutifully silent as we safely crossed the junction. Then, 'Well, Mummy? Are you?'

I stalled again – mentally that is. 'Why do you ask?' I gently queried.

Being December and with the usual preparations and run up to Christmas, he proceeded to tell me that his class were learning about Mary who had a 'special baby'. 'She was a virgin,' he explained. So because I had often called my beloved son 'my special baby', he had wondered if I too was a virgin!

It was my turn for an explanation. 'You know that Daddy is the new commander of the squadron – well, he thinks he's a god – and even talks like one!' This was met with silence. 'In fact, sweetheart, I am a bit of a disappointment to Daddy.' It was still quiet in the back. I pressed on, 'Mary's son was special, and He was the Son of God. So although Daddy thinks he's a god, I am afraid that you're not a son of god and I am not a virgin Mummy! You are still my special baby though.'

GOD'S ACTION MEN

My young son had invited one of his classmates back to tea and I was driving them home after school. His friend lived locally and his family had no connection with the Royal Air Force.

The two of them were chatting animatedly as we passed the Base on the way to our home in the next village. His friend was looking out of the window at the gate guards in their blue RAF uniforms when I heard my son pipe up, 'Those are God's Action Men you know!'

CHILDREN CAN BE HELPFUL

A warrant officer on the squadron had just died and my husband, our only child (a 4-year-old boy) and I had called in to see his widow to offer our support. She invited us into her sitting room and, just as she was in the middle of telling us about the plans that her husband had made for the garden, the doorbell rang.

It was one of the flight commanders, who had come to help her arrange her husband's funeral. My husband and son went sombrely with him into the kitchen while the wife continued to recount all of her husband's ideas for the garden. She was determined to fulfil his ambition by herself.

Quite suddenly, we were all aware of my son's voice talking loudly to the Flight Commander. As he spoke boldly about himself, with obvious exaggeration here and there, our smiles turned to muted laughter. Eventually his story-telling exceeded even his normal level of imagination, 'You know I've got three brothers, a thirty-year-old who lives next door, plus two others, one black and one white, who live in London.'

Was it his way of diffusing an uncomfortable atmosphere?

SLEEPING WITH THE GROOM

In the early 1970s a group of us had been invited down from Coltishall to the Summer Ball at Wyton. When we arrived we went for pre-drinks in the room of a friend who lived in the Mess. I must have had a busy day because after a glass of champagne I thought it would be a good idea to have a little bit of a lie down to make sure I would last through the night of partying that was ahead. One of our friends had brought their baby boy in his carry cot, so I went to the room where the baby was (this was the 1970s; we didn't see anything wrong with that at the time). The carry cot was in the middle of the bed, so I arranged myself in my fancy ball gown round the baby so that I didn't disturb him.

My little nap lasted longer than I expected, for the next thing I knew my husband was gently waking me up to get back on the bus to go home. I had missed the whole Summer Ball, but I have always referred to the event as the best-dressed sleep I have ever had.

Roll on nearly thirty years and my husband and I are guests at the baby's wedding. At the reception the speeches were in full flow and I suggested to my husband that the other guests might be amused to hear about the time I slept with the bridegroom. He assured me this was not a good idea, and on reflection I am sure he was right.

THE TELEPHONE CALL

In the late 1980s my husband became Station Commander. A large number of retired air marshals lived in the local area. Some of these retired worthies were never backwards in coming forwards to give any shiny new station commander the benefit of their own perceived wisdom and experience on how a Station should be run. There was one particular senior officer so well known for passing on such wisdom that my husband had been warned what to expect when he took command of the station with the sound advice to 'just ignore the old boy'!

Not long after our arrival at the Base, we were sitting as a family in the living room after dinner when our 16-year-old daughter, home from school and constantly on the phone to one friend or the other, rushed down the corridor to answer yet another call. She suddenly reappeared in the room and said to her father, 'Dad it's for you, it's that Air Marshal.' My husband got to his feet, let out a number of expletives that even I had not heard him utter before, and ended with, 'What does the silly old b... want this time?' – whereupon our daughter magically produced the cordless phone from behind her back and handed it to her now embarrassed father. It is almost certain the Air Marshal had heard every word, because that was the last call we ever received from him.

A GRAVE SITUATION

What do you do when your child cries, 'I think Hammy is dead!' You are in the middle of cleaning and packing up the house, the removal men are due in a couple of days and now, of all times, the pet hamster chooses to expire.

The immediate soothing and consolatory words will include something like, 'We'll make him a grave at the bottom of the garden, sweetheart. Would you like to choose a special place?' But the unexpected happens and your Little Darling is one step ahead

62

of you, knowing full well that you are on the move. 'We can't just leave him,' she wails.

We Service parents are nothing if not resourceful when pushed into awkward corners. My husband comes to the rescue. 'I'll tell you what – why don't we give Hammy a really nice burial with full military honours and inter him in one of our lovely big flower pots – then he can come with us!'

This was not accepted instantly. A tear-stained face asks, 'What does "inter" mean?'

So it was all arranged and a large terracotta pot of geraniums was ceremoniously moved from Medmenham to Cranwell ... then to Wyton. Thereafter, this hefty grave was reverently moved from pillar to post – until finally, after daughter started at boarding school, it was rather irreverently emptied on top of a compost heap!

4

Hostess With the Mostest

AN EARLY DINNER GUEST

During my husband's tenure as CO of a large North Yorkshire airfield, we invited the local MP for dinner on a Sunday evening before he left the constituency to head south to London. Being the weekend I had decided to do the cooking myself and, with the VIP guest being invited at '7.30 for 8.00 pm', at seven o'clock (dressed in jeans and T-shirt) I left the meal bubbling away under the watchful eye of my housekeeper and steward and went up to change.

As I stripped off to jump in the shower, my husband, wrapped in a towel, glanced out of the upstairs window to see an RAF police car drawing up, the escort for our distinguished guest. Now it is a well-known fact that, in times of crisis, a woman's reactions are much quicker than a man's. I snatched the nearest dress in the wardrobe, dragged a comb through my hair and shot down the stairs, arriving at the bottom at exactly the same moment as the politician turned from being divested of his coat.

As I welcomed him, slightly breathlessly, to our home he replied, 'I think I might be a little early?'

'Oh no,' I replied (through gritted teeth and smiling sweetly), 'not at all' and I continued to make small talk until my husband arrived to take over. I then politely withdrew through the kitchen, where the staff were doubled-up in hysterics, and back upstairs to apply make-up. Of course, I could hardly change the dress!

The message went out to our RAF Station family: 'Should you invite xxx for dinner, beware!'

CULINARY CAUTION

As a young newly-wed, the day came when I was destined to give my first dinner party, or perhaps I should say, buffet supper party since my husband had decided it would be nice to invite all his work colleagues and their wives – 25 people in all.

Since it was winter, I decided that a nice, warming chilli-con-carne with accompanying rice, garlic bread and salad would be just the ticket. I had not made one before but remembered having a similar tasty dish at someone's house a while before. I found a recipe and set to work making the chilli, only to discover that I was almost out of chilli powder. Time was marching on and, in those days, I hadn't realised that cooking often took somewhat longer to complete than one expected. The shops would be shutting soon but, no problem, there was a little shop down the road run by an Asian family that stayed open until late and would be sure to have chilli powder. The item was duly purchased and I continued with the recipe multiplying the ingredients (the recipe was for four people) as I went along.

Shortly before the guests arrived, I invited my husband to sample my simmering marvel. He swallowed a good spoonful then started to dance round the kitchen shouting, 'It's hot, it's hot!'

'Well, let it cool for a minute,' I replied, nonplussed.

'No, no, it's not that sort of hot,' he retorted. I couldn't think what he meant so, after blowing on a teaspoonful to cool it, I popped it in my mouth. As I swallowed, a fire immediately began to blaze on my tongue, in my throat, then in the roof of my mouth. Everything seemed to glow with the heat and I could feel my cheeks going red. After knocking back several glasses of water (though something in my head said I shouldn't), the fire gradually subsided leaving a distinct tingling sensation.

'You can't give them this!' said my husband. 'They'll be drinking me out of house and home.' There was only one thing I could think of to do in the time available. I tipped the chilli-con-carne into a colander and gave it a good swirl around under the tap before replacing it in a dish. Then I quickly made some stock with beef Oxo cubes, added it to the chilli, stirred thoroughly and popped the dish into the oven to warm through. What had gone wrong? My Asian chilli powder must have been super-strength and not exactly what the recipe had in mind or had I miscalculated when increasing the quantity? The doorbell rang and our first guests arrived.

From that day, I have been nervous of tasting chilli-con-carne and – moral of tale – always try out recipes before using them for dinner parties. Perhaps, though, I had the last laugh since one of the guests complimented me on my chilli dish and asked if she could have the recipe! I warned her about strong chilli powder but hadn't the courage to tell her about the 'rinsing under the tap' bit.

SHERRY MORNING

I was living in quarters at South Cerney in Gloucestershire and newly married. All the quarters looked exactly the same, same furniture, same front doors, same everything. I received an invitation from the Squadron Commander's wife, whom I had not met, to a sherry morning (those were the days!) and I duly accepted. On the day of the sherry morning (they never seemed to be called parties did they?) it was raining heavily and I set off with umbrella held down against the wind and rain and rang the doorbell of the quarter. I was ushered in and given my first glass of sherry and then some canapés and so the morning progressed.

After a while, I looked around the room and thought, 'I know so few people here, in fact I don't know anyone.' I had met several members of our squadron before, but none of them was here. 'How odd,' thought I.

Then, horror of horrors, as the rain cleared and I could see the other married quarters across the road, I recognised several faces in the front room window of the house opposite. I had gone to the wrong sherry morning! I made my apologies to the lady of the house and wended my way.

THRIFT SHOP TASTE

We were known for our parties! One year we invited our Station Commander and his wife, plus a whole host of friends, to a 'bad taste' party. This prompted one of our younger female invitees to go to the ultimate lengths to satisfy the theme. She went to the Thrift Shop to seek out and buy the dress she knew had been discarded there by the CO's wife. She then wore it to the party making no secret of its origin. This was perhaps not the most career-enhancing move she could have come up with for her husband, but it did give rise to much hilarity at the time.

'How d'you *know* it was your dress?'

CAN'T COOK

I have a friend who did not cook. Really, did not cook and was not interested in cooking. Her interests lay with breeding horses and dogs. Her husband on the other hand, was the domestic god of culinary delights – he was master in the kitchen, an arrangement that suited them both.

It so happened he had to go away on detachment, and so her friends rallied round, and delicious hot food kept her body and soul together. However, in time a large cloud gathered over her conscience about returning her friends' hospitality; so she wrote to her husband and explained the dilemma.

'No problem,' he replied. 'A roast is the best and easiest dish to serve and guess what, it can all be cooked in the oven,' sending her a complete list of instructions in shopping, preparing and cooking the meal.

Delighted with this news, all her friends were invited round to enjoy a roast. All the bits and pieces were placed in the oven and the guests made merry with pre-dinner drinks. The trusty 'pinger' on the oven told her that the meal was absolutely ready and all the guests seated themselves around the table in amiable anticipation.

Funny though, as she made towards the kitchen, where was the wonderful aroma that normally accompanies a roast dinner? Nothing. Her darling husband had omitted 'Turn on the oven' from the list of instructions. Oops!

NEXT MONDAY

While living in Germany with the army, the Padre and his wife invited us for supper on a Monday night. They lived quite close to us so, on the appointed evening, my husband and I walked across the road to their quarter. The Padre's daughter answered our knock.

'Hello,' she said politely through a narrowly opened door. We looked at one another.

'You are expecting us for supper, aren't you?'

'Oh, yes,' she replied. 'Next Monday.'

We crawled back across the road feeling very embarrassed!

Better than being a week late though.

THE MP'S SKIRT

When my husband was Station Commander he was asked to host a visit and dinner for MPs who were investigating forces' pay and conditions. Not to be outdone by the army, who had previously hosted the same MPs, we decided to soften the visit by using our residence rather than the austere Officers' Mess for dinner and accommodation.

The Mess Chef and stewards were duly summoned to help and, after much primping, polishing and cooking, the house was all set for the visit. The guests arrived. It was the custom for the steward to take their cases to the bedrooms and offer to unpack and press any garments that were required. One rather loud lady MP who held court all the time and smoked non-stop told the steward to unpack her skirt and give it a press. This was duly done and the skirt was returned to her room.

Later that evening catching up with the steward I asked how things were going and he replied, 'Fine thank you Ma'am, but that's the first time I have had my hand up an MP's skirt.'

NIGERIAN SUPPER PARTY

We were at Bracknell in 1985 – Staff College, fantastic parties, meeting many overseas students. We lived next door to a lovely Nigerian couple and their family who asked us, with our two children, round for a drink one evening. Expecting just a drink or two, I made sure our children had eaten before we went. Imagine my surprise to find a dining table absolutely groaning with their local delicacies! It was all so delicious and we forced ourselves to chomp through it with a gracious smile – all four of us, eating for England!

AT HOME CARD

While we were serving in NATO in the 1990s we had a series of dinner parties and to one we invited an unaccompanied German officer with the usual invitation to join 'Mrs Bloggs, At Home'. We found out later, through his colonel, that it had apparently caused him great anxiety, because he thought he was being invited to a cosy dinner for two! Fortunately he had sought the advice of an English colleague who explained that this was an idiosyncratic British way of inviting guests to dinner – and not to worry as the Boss would be there and several other couples too! He was mightily relieved – but it was a shame – he was very good looking!

THE DINNER BELL

We had been invited to the Station Commander's for dinner. One of the guests was unable to make it at the last moment and so the dining table seating plan had been rearranged. This meant that a squadron leader with a wicked sense of humour was now sitting in the Station Commander's usual place. The residence was such that there was a bell press under the carpet, which was used by the Station Commander to summon the steward for more drinks or to clear dishes after a course.

This particular Station Commander was very punctilious, such that you could always expect your standard issue G&T on arrival and then your regulation two drinks with the meal. Discovering that he had control of the bell, the mischievous Squadron Leader made sure the drinks kept coming on a very regular basis and, as there were several non-military guests present, the Station Commander was unable to gainsay this apparent generosity.

ONE GLASS TOO MANY

My husband was posted to RAF Upavon in the mid 1980s. We lived in quarters but felt we should get to know some of the locals. Having invited a few to dinner, we were eight around our limited dining table. I sat next to a delightful – if expansive – gentleman. He was an enthusiastic Tiger Moth pilot and ex-Para, recounting tales of his exploits and demonstrating with flailing hands the various manoeuvres he had performed over the years to escape life-threatening situations.

But then, his glass of red wine got in the way and the contents landed on me. I quickly nipped upstairs to change my clothes, and sat down again. Then the second glass landed in my lap ... a swift change of trousers before I returned in an attempt to enjoy my meal. When the third glass of wine descended on me I decided to just stick with it – never knowing if it might happen again. It didn't – but at least I was prepared!!

APPELLATION CONTRÔLLÉE

In the 1970s there was a period when the Services were very badly paid (weren't they always!), and we had been introduced to wine making by my father, something many of us undertook to help retain some sort of party capability, as buying wine was too expensive. Well, we went into quantity production – probably could have set up a business, except that we drank it too quickly. Our airing cupboard was a source of bubbling and hiccups as this liquid fermented and became wine. It was passable stuff, generally good for punch or Gluhwein, but one was always conscious of its origin.

When my husband was commanding his squadron we had a dinner party with the Station Commander as principal guest – an essential career-promoting move. He too was a wine maker, and unbeknown to me he brought a large bottle as a dinner gift. To make the most of the evening my husband served this wine with the main course, from the unlabelled bottles usual to us all. Having sipped some of the wine, I asked my husband why he had served such awful stuff! He knew its source and could tell the CO had recognised his own bottle; not a relaxing evening after that. Oh dear.

RUNNING WATER

The plumbing in our married quarter left a lot to be desired. On one occasion an evening dinner guest, who was due to stay overnight, arrived in the late afternoon in time for the usual cup of tea before a bath and changing. We exchanged pleasantries in the lounge then I showed him to his room, pointing out the bathroom, etc. A few minutes later he appeared downstairs rather red faced to say he could get no water in his room – sure enough, there was no water available anywhere in the house except in the kitchen.

Chef was valiantly preparing dinner for twenty people with only cold water from the mains tap. Undaunted, we reverted to Victorian principles and provided a jug of hot water for washing and several buckets of cold water for the toilets. The duty plumber had been contacted but, typically, was 'unavailable' until the morning.

Our dinner guests arrived: the local MP, several local dignitaries, a High Court judge, a couple of senior officers and their wives. All were discreetly told that the facilities would be VERY basic for the evening. There were some strange and bewildered looks. Drinks and canapés were served, the men gradually gravitating to one end of the room whereupon two took off their dinner jackets and disappeared with my husband. In the space of five minutes there was not a man left in the room. They were all up in the attic climbing over the cobweb-festooned pipework and pronouncing that it was like the 'Good ship Lollipop'. Much banging, tweaking, shouting up and down the stairs, and turning on and off of various taps resulted in a triumphant shout as normal water service was resumed.

Eight male strangers in dicky bows descended from the attic, washed their hands in warm water, brushed themselves down, put on their jackets and, looking extremely self-satisfied, sat down to dinner. Thereafter, conversation was easy and animated!

THE DUTY DINNER PARTY

The PSO's wife was a bundle of nerves. Her husband had declared that they couldn't put it off any longer; they simply had to invite the Boss for dinner. It was the mid 1970s at HQ RAF Germany and it had to be a 'black tie do'.

Her stress levels soared. Everyone knew what a difficult and fussy person the Air Marshal was, not least her husband who was frequently fraught himself. Mrs Air Marshal, although charming, had lived a colonial life and, living in their smart 'residence', being pampered by staff came as naturally to her as to her husband.

The dinner party would require careful planning, selecting the menu, the balance of flavours and textures and, of course, the right guests for animated conversation. Oh yes, there was a lot to think about. She would have to polish the silver. Should she have mats, or the use the damask tablecloth that was her mother's? Then there were the flowers; she was hopeless at doing table arrangements. 'What on earth shall I cook? I shall have to practise.'

'We'll do it together,' her husband soothed. 'I tell you what, I'll get the ADC and his wife to come for supper and we can do a run through, wine and everything. He will also know what the Air Marshal's particular likes and dislikes are.'

She was already thinking. 'I'll do that lemon soufflé – I haven't done it since we moved to Rheindahlen.'

The trial supper went well and the ADC's wife thought the soufflé was a triumph, light and tangy and the perfect finale for the dinner. They discussed the prospective guests, who would be carefully chosen and briefed on their principal guest.

The evening arrived and everything was ready. The individual soufflés had been carefully made in the morning. Later the silicon paper had been removed to reveal perfect little specimens that were decorated with lemon rind. 'This is the first and last dinner party,' the wife warned her PSO husband. 'It's just too stressful!'

'Don't worry, dear. At least it won't be hanging over our heads any more.'

The candles were lit and the guests arrived ten minutes early, as briefed. Time for a stiff drink before the Air Marshal's Rover purred up to the door.

The dinner was going well, and the PSO's wife relaxed. It was all over bar the dessert and she was perfectly confident that it would be well received. As she brought the pretty lemon soufflés out of the kitchen and carefully placed them in front of her guests, there were complimentary murmurs around the table.

The first mouthfuls were being savoured when, quite suddenly, the Air Marshal enquired, 'Do you have a Kenwood or a Sunbeam?' Everybody stopped eating.

'Sorry? A food-mixer you mean?' The PSO's wife looked puzzled.

'Yes. Which one did you use to make this marvellous concoction?'

'A Sunbeam, actually.'

The Air Marshal was looking somewhat serious as he inspected his dessert spoon. 'I suspect this little devil must be a Sunbeam screw then.'

There was a horrified silence and the PSO rose. 'I ... I'm dreadfully sorry, Sir. How awful...'

'Goodness, don't worry. These things happen. It is a simply delicious soufflé, never tasted better. Congratulations, my dear.' He smiled broadly and put another spoonful into his mouth. 'Oh dear.' All the guests were alert. 'Excuse me!' The Air Marshal delicately put a finger and thumb to his lips while the assembled dinner guests, like waxwork figures, looked on transfixed. The only sound was the tinkle of a small nut and a bolt as they landed on his side plate.

The PSO's wife nearly passed out.

'Darling, that's enough!' The Air Marshal's wife smiled benevolently at her husband, 'He's up to his trickery again.'

TACEVAL AT VALLEY

We had just arrived at RAF Valley and, not surprisingly perhaps, the station's personnel wanted to find out what the new couple in the big house were like. Valley, being a training establishment, was heavily populated with students who still had that certain *joie de vivre* that seems to diminish with responsibility.

One Friday night I got a call from the bar, telling me to stand by for a 'Taceval' by one of the courses. The evening went well – particularly when our large store of 60s and 70s vinyl records was discovered. Our Springer pup 'Megan' was literally lapping up all the attention.

The following Monday we received the Taceval report, duly graded. We got top marks for the arrival, including speed of beer and food; however, in the Comments column it was noted that 'Megan's welcome was overwhelming, but tongues on a first date were a bit OTT'.

AN INTERESTING STARTER

We were hosting a dinner for twelve in the Station Commander's residence. I returned from work in time for a quick change and a final check of the seating plan. The table had been beautifully prepared by our housekeeper and I was looking forward to a delicious dinner. My flowers looked lovely and, as I finished laying out the name cards, I felt quite proud, that is until I realised that I still had two cards left in my hand. Shock horror – the table was laid for only ten!

I rushed into the kitchen to discuss with chef – all was not lost.

The main course and pudding could be stretched but the starter was an individual creation of seafood in filo pastry and there were no spares. The table was hastily re-laid while I did a mad dash to the 24-hour Tesco up the road to purchase something that resembled our elegant starter.

On my return I just had time to brief my husband to make no comment on the size, presentation or taste of his starter as it was unique! It was a culinary masterpiece – and the best-dressed sausage roll he had ever eaten.

BASIC COOKING

We were fairly newly married and living in our first married quarter. My husband invited a former colleague, with whom he had worked in Aden, to come and give a lecture to a course he was running, also suggesting that he bring his wife and stay the night with us.

On the due evening I prepared a steak and kidney supper (I couldn't cope with pastry for a pie) but as I hadn't prepared the kidneys as well as I might, it wasn't a raging success. Of course, our guests were too polite to say anything (I wish I could say the same about my husband) but the evening passed pleasantly enough.

The next morning while the men and I went off to work, the wife took herself off into the local city to see the sights. When we met up again later in the day I was delighted to be given a little 'thank you' gift but imagine my reaction when I unwrapped a book – *Good Housekeeping Basic Cookery (1969)*!

RED SETTER SETBACK

At my insistence we had obtained a mad Irish Setter to keep me company during my husband's imminent posting on a 13-month unaccompanied tour to Sharjah. He was a lovely, loving dog but unfortunately had very little between his ears!

After coping with simple suppers, I had graduated to dinner parties. Towards the end of one particular dinner party, I was serving coffee and the Boss's wife insisted we let in our pet which had been locked away in the kitchen. My husband duly obliged but, in its excitement, the dog took off and landed in the lap of the Boss's wife at precisely the same moment as I handed her a cup of coffee.

My husband swears this put his career back several years. It has always been my fault.

SOAP STORY

When my husband became Squadron Commander I gave up my teaching job in Hertfordshire to support him and his squadron. However, it soon became evident that with two school fees and a large mortgage to pay I would need to get back to work.

I was very lucky and landed myself a head of department teaching job in Lincoln, the only problem being that it was a good 20-mile drive away. I was concerned that I would not be able to cope with being the boss's wife, with all the social commitments that that involved, while teaching at the same time. However, I convinced myself that with good organisation I could cope.

Dinner parties were organised with military precision; desserts were made and frozen during weekday evenings, vegetables prepared before going to work and, where possible, the main course made ready to cook on my return. Fortunately I had a marvellous cleaner who used to work in the Mess and knew how to polish the silver and make the house gleam while I was away.

One Friday I left for work with the table set for ten and the meal almost ready to go in the oven. I rushed home through traffic queues and across the fens. The house looked immaculate thanks to the cleaner, I checked the meal, and found time for a bath (RAF married quarters had no showers in those days). I had time to relax and to pour myself a drink hoping that my husband would be pleased with all my efforts.

I was ready with 10 minutes to spare before the guests arrived, but there was no sign of my husband. I should have known, it was Friday night and he would be at the beer call. He finally arrived just a few minutes before the guests, had a quick fighter pilot shower (underarm spray with deodorant) and changed. Then much to my annoyance he proceeded to do an inspection of the house. He finally went into the loo, checked towels, mirror, loo paper, etc and came out brandishing a rather cracked tired-looking bar of soap saying, 'Can't we do better than this?'

You can imagine my reaction, I could have killed him. It was at that moment the doorbell rang, the first guests arrived and I put on a smile through gritted teeth. I knew I would have slipped up somewhere.

5

Far Flung Places

LUGGAGE LINGERIE

Many years ago a friend of ours was stationed with his family in East Africa. On one occasion he and his crew were tasked to take an aircraft back to the UK for servicing. Seeing this as a shopping opportunity, his wife got together with the other wives and presented him with a large and diverse order for lingerie from Marks & Spencer.

He duly completed this somewhat onerous task but, on his return through customs in Nairobi, he was unexpectedly stopped by a customs officer. The officer proceeded to open up all his bags, displaying a large range of pretty underwear. He made his inspection in silence until eventually, looking our friend in the eye, he said, 'Enjoy your weekend, sir!'

TROUBLE ON BOARD

Life in Singapore in the 1960s had many a good side. Wives were able to 'indulge', as it was called, on Royal Air Force flights. It meant that if there was a spare seat on a transport aircraft going practically anywhere, one could apply for and use it, almost free. This would sometimes be to England on a VC10, or anywhere one fancied.

My friend Maria, whose husband worked with mine on 103 Squadron, decided we would go shopping in Hong Kong.

Husbands duly filled in the indulgence forms and, before we knew it, we were off aboard a Hastings aircraft.

We had a high old time shopping. Unfortunately we missed the return indulgence flight to Singapore and had to pay to get back by civilian aircraft. The aircraft landed en route at Kota Kinabalu and a lot of very drunken lumberjacks and oil workers boarded. Apart from the stewardess, Maria and I were the only females on board. Suddenly an argument broke out, and then a fight. We were petrified. I had visions of a hole being punched in the side of the aircraft and us all being sucked out!

The stewardess approached us and said, 'With the captain's compliments, would you like to join him up front?' (one was able to go up onto the flightdeck in those days). We grabbed our little overnight bags and headed towards the front of the aircraft to be seated in the captain's cabin, on little fold-down seats just behind him. As we approached the airport at Singapore there was the wonderful sight of thousands of lights – even in those bygone days. We heard the captain radio ahead to the airport saying that he had 'trouble on board'. However, we landed safely and I thanked him for his kindness and protection.

'After you, ladies,' he said, ushering us ahead down the steps of the aircraft. A moment later, Maria and I were grabbed under our elbows by the Singapore police and lifted from the bottom step, straight into the arrival shed, under armed guard. The stewardess came rushing across to the police and called out, 'No! These ladies are not the "trouble" – we have drunks on board!'

Nonetheless we were taken into customs and thoroughly searched. Unfortunately I had a copy of *Playboy* magazine in my suitcase – the squadron had asked for a copy for their crew room! (This publication was forbidden in Singapore at the time, but readily available in Hong Kong.) Thank goodness things were soon sorted out and we ran into the arms of our very worried husbands who had been watching our 'arrest' through the windows of Changi airport.

The offending magazine was confiscated by Singapore customs

and our husbands' names, ranks and numbers were taken, as well as my passport number etc. For weeks afterwards I was afraid to open our local newspaper, *The Straits Times*, fearing that I might see the headline 'British officer's wife accused of importing pornographic literature'!

THE VICAR'S WIFE

My husband and I had just arrived in Washington DC for his tour at the embassy. My first introduction to the embassy wives was at a coffee morning not long after. I have to admit I found most of them a little starchy, but saw a very nice homely, friendly-looking lady in a floral print dress, so I went over to talk to her. She was interested to know how long I had been in DC, did I like the house, etc, and was my husband service or diplomatic corps. I said that he was in the Royal Air Force and then politely enquired about her. She told me she was the minister's wife.

Later that evening I was telling my husband about my day, and mentioned how surprised I was that they had a vicar at the embassy – presumably for our pastoral care. No, he assured me, there was no vicar. I said that there was, as I had met his wife, and that she had told me she was the minister's wife. My husband chuckled, and then explained he was not THAT sort of minister, more the very, very senior political kind! Thank goodness I hadn't asked her what denomination he was.

Actually, she'd have made a lovely vicar's wife!

THE COST OF LIVING

We were in Texas, on an exchange tour with the USAF during the 1970s, surrounded by the rich spoils of American living, what more could one want from life?

However, while we were there, MoD decided to review the Local

Overseas Allowance – the daily allowance we were paid to compensate us for the higher cost of living in the USA; this was quite high, especially with a continually falling pound/dollar exchange rate. The study consisted of a direct comparison of the prices of everyday items in England and the USA. To this end we were sent a list of over 100 commodities to price locally.

The list consisted exclusively of food and household goods found in England. So we set about trying to find and price a leg of lamb (Texas being the home of American beef), a jar of gooseberry jam (Americans had not heard of gooseberries let alone jam), a one-pound unsliced loaf of white bread (plain, blue- and pink-coloured sliced were on the shelves, but certainly nothing unsliced). The whole exercise was completely farcical.

MOVERS AND SHAKERS

'We're on the move again!' There is always much anticipation and excitement in the family when a new posting is announced. If the posting is to be overseas there are inoculations to consider and I well remember those injections – cholera being the most painful. Our skin seemed to be peppered with needles the size of elephant legs!

In a bygone era, packing the house was much more straightforward. For a start we had far fewer belongings, which made life less complicated. All our clothes and knick-knacks would be packed into cardboard boxes. Quarters in those days were equipped with beautiful furniture, curtains, crystal, china, bed linens – the lot. It was all carefully listed on an official inventory, which had to be checked and accounted for on 'Marching In' and 'Marching Out'. If we had been lucky enough to have had servants or maids while living in some outpost or other, then the cleaning would all be taken care of. On the other hand, if we were moving out of a quarter in the UK that was another matter entirely.

In later years one accumulated 'clutter' and this all had to be sorted and cleared. The charity shops did well, as did our friends who were bequeathed many half-empty bottles of booze! The cleaning of the house was carried out by a series of eliminations. First, spare rooms not in use were cleaned from top to bottom and then locked up. Similarly, loos surplus to requirements would also be cleaned and locked, leaving just one in service. Curtains were washed and ironed, carpets cleaned, and the garden and sheds tidied up. By far the worst chore was cleaning the cooker. It had to be taken apart and cleaned to within an inch of its life, then carefully covered with tea towels – never to be used again. The camping gear would be brought into service to keep us going in the final week, and thank goodness for good friends who would become a welcome source of nourishment, helping to feed us until we left.

Another major consideration when moving abroad was what items would be put into a storage depot for the duration. Enormous thought went into this selection, but even so, two years on, when it was delivered to your new abode, it was normally clear that you were utterly insane to have collected and kept such rubbish!

The last chore after the removal men had loaded up the lorries was to clean the kitchen floor, and finally reverse out of the back door on hands and knees. Then those filthy cleaning clothes would be dumped in the dustbin. A sparkling house was ready for inspection!

It is fair to say that often the same degree of cleanliness was not found at the next quarter!

Having moved so many times, I can honestly say that moving from America back to the UK was the best experience. No 'Cif' or rubber gloves were required. Everything was efficiently done for you. I could dress up and go out to lunch with friends – every day while the whole packing and cleaning process was going on – then return to the house, painted nails intact, just as the last packing cases were being eased into a wagon. They packed absolutely everything; a peanut butter sandwich even once made it back to England!

FRIENDSHIPS FOR LIFE

You know, living abroad with young children, we were so lucky in more ways than one. However, the biggest issue in my opinion was finding a good babysitter and a decent hairdresser.

A good babysitter was like gold dust, and usually had to be shared. Sometimes we would double up with friends, if there was a big 'Do' in the Mess. Often, prior to giving a dinner party, children would be off-loaded next door for 'sleep-overs' (modern phrase) which would ease the 4 am wash-up (in the days before dish-washers) and allow a vaguely leisurely morning rise.

But the best thing was having a long weekend away from the little darlings by taking turns to have each other's children. A few days of bliss was enough to restore one's equilibrium and sense of humour, and actually, halfway through the last day, one couldn't wait to be with the children again. Friendships were so valuable, accepting us, our young children, warts and all, without reservation.

Most importantly, these friendships are for life. Maybe it is just a card at Christmas, but laughter, hugs and tears ensue when reunions take place and time soon seems immaterial.

AN AMERICAN IN CANADA

We left England on our exchange tour to Canada on one of those glorious spring days when green shoots were on the trees and the daffodils were beginning to show their splendour. In contrast we arrived in Canada with temperatures 20 degrees below zero. The snow was piled metres high and, although we had on our UK overcoats and sturdiest shoes, we were totally unprepared for the conditions we encountered.

After a few days being briefed by the High Commission in Ottawa we travelled to Bagotville in northern Quebec where we stayed in a very small apartment hotel while trying to find a house to rent. Our two children were very young, and when my husband set off to work with the car each morning I was left wondering how to fill my day. It was impossible to walk outside because of the cold and the wind chill factor, and besides, I would have needed a sledge to transport the children. I was beginning to feel very lonely and homesick.

However, in the next apartment was an American family from the Deep South of Louisiana. They had four children a little older that our two, and they had also recently arrived for an exchange posting with the Canadians. We made contact and I explained that we were from England and also on exchange. After comparing notes about weather and housing we let the children play together. I could never quite understand what my new-found friend was actually saying because her American accent was very strong and she seemed to chew gum most of the time. After a few days I realised that she kept her rollers in her hair all day until her husband returned from work, and that she spent her day watching the soaps on television. The only problem was that Quebec is a totally French-speaking province and the only TV we could get was in French, so although she watched it continually, she could probably understand very little of it.

Over coffee one day I asked her how they had travelled to Canada from America, and she explained that they had driven all the way, taking several days to complete the journey. She then turned to me and said, 'Ya'll from England, ya'll drive here?' I said no, we had not driven here, and before I could say more she asked, 'Ya'll come bah train?' I had not got the heart to explain where England was, or to point out the small problem of the Atlantic Ocean lying in between, so I replied politely that we had come by air.

Decades later G.W. Bush displayed a similar grasp of world geography.

GEOGRAPHY LESSON

A posting to the Supreme Headquarters Allied Powers Europe (SHAPE) near Mons in Belgium was a multicultural experience. Fairly early on in our tour I met an American wife who seemed like a fish out of water. Europe was so different from the United States, she explained. She had hardly settled in and, on one occasion, her eyes filling with tears, she confided, 'I have found it really difficult adjusting to life here in France.'

'You mean Belgium, not France,' I remarked.

'Oh, I thought Belgium was in France.' She was truly surprised.

Perhaps there was some consolation in my enlightenment!

SHOPPING IN THE EASTERN BLOC

At the height of the Cold War my husband and I visited West Berlin and one day went through the border to the East. Being a military officer he was obliged to wear his uniform, which caused great interest from the locals. We would go into an empty shop and suddenly find ourselves surrounded by loads of people who were trying not to be noticed. We took ourselves into a department store, believing that it would be stocked full of sports gear – there was nothing. We had never seen such empty shelves. But the Meissen shop was a different story!

The well-tried procedure was to buy your illegal East German marks from the '*Zoo*' (tube station) in West Berlin and then make the journey through Check Point Charlie to the Meissen shop in East Berlin. You would buy your china and then go back through Check Point Charlie in the hope that no one would check your car. Your husband had to go and hand back the paperwork that had been given to him before going through and, on this occasion, while waiting for him to return, I saw that he was accompanied by an East German policeman. My heart went into overdrive and I started to imagine the prison that we would be dragged off to.

However, all he wanted was some paperwork that my husband had forgotten!

That was our last visit to East Berlin.

THE ASTRONAUT

My husband had just started a tour working at the British Embassy in Washington DC, and we were to have our first big dinner party. When my husband asked if an unexpected female guest could come along, the answer was, of course, 'Yes,' but I had no chance to ask anything about who she was, where she was from, etc.

A very pretty young lady in her early thirties turned up. The first opportunity I had to talk to her was at the dining table. Thinking I had a safe opening line, I asked, 'So what do you do?'

Complete silence descended around the table. My husband was just too far away to kick me, but he quickly interjected, 'She is a Colonel in the United States Air Force, darling,' with a look – that I ignored – which said, 'Stop digging!'

'Oh,' I continued, 'how interesting, and what do you do in the Air Force?'

The young lady replied, 'Well, my first degree was in engineering, but since I love flying I decided to go through test-pilot school soon after I graduated.'

Quickly trying to change tack, I asked, 'So how did you meet your husband?'

'I met him on the first astronaut training course to include women.'

By now utterly lost for words, I moved on to what I thought was safer ground. 'And do you have a family?' (I was thinking to myself, 'Of course not, where would she have found the time, it's just not possible.')

'Yes,' came the reply. 'We have two children. Unfortunately we didn't both make it through astronaut training, so my husband elected to stay at home and be the house-husband.'

Later that evening, when we fell into bed, my husband, who was a fighter pilot in the RAF, rolled over, turned off the light and said, 'God, that woman made me feel so inadequate!'

CHRISTMAS LETTER FROM HARARE

What have we been up to? Not a lot really. It's been a great year because lots of friends have been out to see us and it's made us feel a bit nearer home! About 70 people have been to stay since February. I'm sure we don't know that many people, but we sent people next door if we didn't recognise them!

We leave Zimbabwe in December with a heavy heart. We've had such a wonderful time here, but we'll be glad to go home to friends and family. We have been working with the army for 3 years now. We have been completely taken over by them and may never be able to return to the RAF. The army have expended hours of hard work inducting us in their ways. We think we've finally passed the course. The army had to give us lessons in army speak. First lesson was AIR HAIR LAIR (Oh hello!) and second was SIGHDOU (When people ask 'Do you shoot?' The answer is SIGHDOU) (YES I DO), I wanted to say CORSIGHDOU, but the army said that wouldn't be acceptable!!! Life is a rich tapestry!

What will be our lasting memories of the year? Will it be taking the dog to the vet? It's not everywhere you have to wait because someone's brought their pet lion in to be de-wormed! Or will it be trying to tell the staff at the local Lion and Cheetah Park that a crocodile has escaped. Then seeing the locals cutting down trees to whack the crocodile till he's really mad and finally trying to push the crocodile backwards through the hole he came out of? Maybe it will be the local newspaper cuttings we've read, berating the police for not coming to work on their own bicycles. 'A policeman not bringing his own bicycle to work is like a farmer going to work without his hoe!'

Some of our guests have had adventures. One group went away

to a safari island, where unfortunately the cook died while they were staying. When they got on the boat to go back to the mainland the safari operators had removed a door and put the dead cook on the door to be transported back to the mainland!

Seriously, we've had a wonderful year. We've done more daring safaris in wilder parts of Zimbabwe. We've stayed in wire netting lodges, so that we were in cages and not the animals. One afternoon we were relaxing on the bed when I saw a large snake crawling up the wire netting, my husband threw a shoe at it as all good hunters do, but we decided we should get help. I finally went to our guide's house and woke him up. He said he would come and then asked me if I could see anything around me. When I said no, he said there had been an elephant right where I was standing just a few moments ago! He came over to the lodge and informed us it was a harmless bush snake, which he then chased off. When we came to fly out (there were no roads to the camp) there was an elephant on the runway, so the manageress of the camp had to try and frighten it off. He eventually moved away, as she was making such a noise, and went to a tree, which he started bashing presumably in a fit of rage! When our airplane took off, he chased us down the runway!

So it is that we leave Zimbabwe having had a wonderful tour, excited about coming home and wondering what excitement our next tour will hold. Have a great Christmas!

FIRST DAY IN BERLIN

As the plane banked slowly the children and I peered out excitedly on the snow-clad city below ... Berlin! It was 6 December 1983 and the very name Berlin conjured up images of spy movies, dastardly Russians, Checkpoint Charlie, and clandestine meetings on forbidding border crossings. It was the middle of the Cold War. No wonder we were all so excited about arriving in this notorious, but fascinatingly beautiful and cultured city. It was like arriving in a living history text book and, being a history teacher, it had a special fascination for me.

We had flown in, via London, direct from the most northerly part of the British Isles, the island of Unst in the Shetland Islands, where we had spent the last 18 months of an RAF tour. On Shetland we had loved the feeling of being on a remote island surrounded by untamed seas, suffused in spectacular wild life and northern Viking culture. Now we were swapping one kind of island for another, for Berlin was an island of western democracy surrounded by the sinister republic of East Germany. It had a wild life of a very different kind – Russian soldiers, the KGB and worst of all, the East German secret police, known as the Stasi. But Berlin could boast one of the most vibrant city cultures in the Western world – the contrast couldn't have been more dramatic.

We had no idea what we were coming to, where we would be living, what the local school was like, who our friends would be – this was long before the era of mobile phones, the Internet and computers. It was certainly very strange to us, as not only was this Berlin, the fabled city, but it was in West Germany, our very first tour abroad, and we knew little about the people or the language – although we did know that they drove on the other side of the road.

My husband had set off in the family car, heaped up with our belongings, to drive alone across Europe. He would have to approach Berlin through a designated road known as 'the corridor', which was patrolled by Russians – it was all part of the Allied Forces Agreement. He would need to negotiate both British and Russian checkpoints at Helmstedt, at the western end of the corridor and then Russian and British checkpoints on entering Berlin. He then had to find his way through an unfamiliar city to the British Air Force Base of RAF Gatow. But we had the utmost faith in him – of course he would be there to meet us – wouldn't he?

We were looking rather lost when a friendly RAF officer, realising it was our first time in Berlin, led us to the families' area where we were to meet my husband. At last we saw him, frantically waving to us from behind the barrier, dressed in uniform, having obviously come straight from work.

That's when I knew we had a problem. His face took on his famous amiable expression of 'It'll be fine,' when it always, most certainly, was not.

'Well, I've had a few problems but I've sorted most of them out, but don't worry, it'll be fine! There are no quarters available on the base until mid January, so we've been given an apartment in the middle of the city until then. It's dead easy to find.'

'What do you mean, "dead easy to find"? You are taking us there aren't you?'

'Well, you see, I would,' he writhed, 'but there is a slight problem. Quite by accident and unwittingly, I seem to have committed a few offences when driving through the corridor, and the military police have taken my driving licence and temporarily withdrawn my permission to drive in Berlin.' He smiled at me weakly.

'What offences?' I asked, my lips drawing into a thin line.

'Well, apparently I shouldn't have been carrying firearms, and I had my shotgun with me. That's when I was arrested by the Russians, when they spotted my gun. It took me quite a while to talk my way out of that one.' Laughing, he continued, 'The military police weren't too happy either. They've confiscated my shotgun for the time being.'

I couldn't believe he was taking it all so lightly. 'Anyway, you can drive to the apartment, it's easy peasy. I was lucky to get the time off to meet you but now I must get back to work.'

'How do you expect me to drive into the middle of a strange city, to a place I don't know, on German roads when I've never even driven on the right before?' I knew I must not let my children down. I had to be strong, courageous and determined. All the qualities needed in a military wife!

'Come on then chaps,' I called, grasping the car keys and the children's hands tightly as I followed him out to the car park.

'That's the spirit!' he called back.

I spoke no German whatsoever, but I could at least point to the address written on a card. His instructions were ringing in my head and I tried not to let the children see how nervous, quite frankly terrified, I was at the prospect of setting off into the middle of Berlin with just my two precious children beside me. I had to keep remembering to keep my side of the car next to the kerb to ensure I was on the correct side of the road. I couldn't believe the situation he had put me into! I could have throttled him as he cheerily waved us on our way.

How on earth was I to find my way in this unknown, snowbound city? What if I drove over to the East by mistake, never be to heard of again in some dreadful Stasi jail!

'Pull yourself together,' I kept muttering to myself. 'You're not stupid, you're an intelligent adult – or an incredibly stupid one to agree to this plan!'

I then hit upon a brilliant tactic that I have used ever since, whenever I have found myself in such a terrifying situation. I thought to myself, 'When would this situation seem like a blessing? In what circumstances would I think myself lucky to be given an unknown address in Berlin and be told to take my children there?' As a military wife, this is so useful – I imagine myself into a far worse situation where I would have to cope, even be glad to cope – and it has always worked. And I certainly hit on the right one for Berlin.

'I know,' I thought, 'if it were in the middle of World War II, when Berlin was under Nazi rule, and I was a Jewish mother needing a safe house in which to hide my children, I'd drive anywhere, whatever the conditions to get them to safety.'

So in my head that's what I became – a mother trying to save her children. With fresh determination I forged ahead through the traffic with a new confidence; so confident in fact that I drove straight over the main crossroads with the Heerstrasse and missed the right turn!

'Blast!' I shouted. 'That's where I should have turned right!'

'Don't worry Mum,' called my daughter sitting up beside me and looking out of the front windscreen intently. 'There's a turning up ahead, look! You can turn round there.' She was pointing to a turning on the left. I slowed down and managed to negotiate the turn more or less correctly. This road wasn't anywhere near so busy but I noticed several people waving at us from the pavement.

'Oh, look how friendly the Berliners are,' I said to the children happily.

'No Mum,' my son shouted frantically from the back. 'You're on the wrong side of the road, that's why they're waving!'

I lurched crazily over to the other verge just before coming face to face with the oncoming traffic. My heart was pumping, so I pulled into the side of the road and stopped. 'I'll just get my bearings a moment,' I giggled nervously. 'That was fun – don't tell Dad mind. He'll just say I'm a hopeless driver.'

We had stopped in front of a rather large gateway with huge forbidding walls surrounding it. The walls were so high you could not see any buildings beyond them. But what we could see were some unfamiliar soldiers looking at us and obviously discussing why we had stopped in their gateway. There were more soldiers patrolling the walls and they were not soldiers we recognised; they were certainly not British, not American, not even French.

'Cor Mum look,' whispered my son conspiratorially. 'They're Russians!'

'Oh my God!' I whispered back. 'Wherever can we be!' My mind began to race. Had I inadvertently driven into the East? Was that possible?

'They are real Russians, aren't they Mum? They've got those big hats on with the red bands,' breathed my son, absolutely beside himself with excitement. One of the soldiers began to walk towards us. I looked his uniform up and down; he was a real Russian all right!

'Where the bloody hell are we?' I began to panic. 'Don't tell Dad I swore!'

'Mum, it must be Spandau jail; remember Dad said we were to turn right just before Spandau?'

Thank heavens for my daughter. I will love her forever and ever! 'Of course darlings,' I breezed, resuming my confident mode. 'That must be where we are. How lucky to see Spandau jail on our first journey in Berlin. Say hello to Rudolf Hess. But I think it's time to go.'

The Russian soldier was now close to the car. Smiling, and waving imperiously at him, I turned the car around and set off back the way we had come.

'Who's Rudolf Hess?' asked an excited son.

'Oh, he's a famous Nazi,' I explained, 'and he's been kept in Spandau jail ever since the war.'

'That's a terribly long time, poor old chap!' observed my daughter. I was touched by her sympathy.

'Well, you see it gives the Russians the perfect excuse to keep bringing their soldiers into West Berlin. So I don't think they'll ever let him go.' Sadly, I was to be proved right.

Once we were on the Heerstrasse the journey wasn't too bad and we eventually found the address on the card and made our way to our apartment on the second floor. We were surprised at how large it was, but had yet to find the best bit – we had a balcony with a wonderful view! In one direction we could look out over Theodor-Heuss Platz, but it was the other direction that was spectacular. We could look right along Kaiserdamm, as far as the eye could see and, as we were to discover, on a clear day we could just make out the Victory Column.

This was the avenue along which the Nazi tanks would have rolled out west, along which the Russian tanks would have advanced when taking over Berlin; it was such a historic view. All along the sides of the street stood the famous, elegant, Victorian-style lampposts designed by none other than Albert Speer himself. They were lovely, and cast an ethereal light all along Kaiserdamm in the gathering gloom. We stood and stared transfixed; Berlin was, indeed, a beautiful city and one with which we were all soon to fall in love.

BE PREPARED

There were several brand new wives joining their husbands on the two Vulcan squadrons sent to Cyprus in early 1969 – I was one of them. We were all very excited girls starting married life in an exotic environment.

For many though, it wasn't really exotic – but it was very different. A lot of us missed our families and friends in the UK and creature comforts like telephones and televisions. I loved it though! I loved the sunshine, heat, colour and the distinctive smells of the island – the sweet jasmine flower at night, the aroma of basil plants, winter oranges and lemons and even the donkeys and goats. I thought I could stay there forever!

However, not long after settling into our village house, my husband brought home a document for me to read. It was to do with evacuation, he explained. I thought that my romantic notion of a lifelong sojourn on Cyprus was about to be cut short. In an emergency situation (it didn't say what), I was to be a designated driver because I had a driving licence and a car to go with it. It would be my job to pick up another wife and her two children, who lived nearby. I should then get us all to the Sovereign Base Area at RAF Akrotiri as fast as possible. Being young and naïve, I found this very frightening. The instructions didn't end there, but listed certain items of food and other things which I should keep at hand – in case of an 'emergency'. Again, at that time, I couldn't envisage quite what was meant, but I followed the recommendations and put together all the appropriate items in one place.

As it happened, I never did experience an 'emergency' and I missed the coup in 1974, when Turkish Forces invaded the island. However, throughout my life, I have never stopped being prepared for an 'emergency', whether it be a shortage of water or warmth, or stuck in a snowy mountain pass, or even on the M25 in a traffic jam. And my food cupboards are always well stocked. You never know!

PHILIPPINE FANS

I spent many years moving with the RAF in the UK before the Queen very kindly decided that my husband should become a military attaché, and we spent three wonderful years living in Singapore, which we found to be a very modern, fast city. From there we moved on to the Philippines which is a rather different world altogether. It was a third world country with strong first world country aspirations.

We lived right in the middle of Manila in a beautiful protected village, surrounded by expats similar to ourselves and super-rich Filipinos. This was completely different from most other parts of the country. We were looked after by numerous staff. Life was rather good, but as with all the jobs of this type we were extremely busy, not to mention the fact that it is a 'twofers' job. Buy one (Defence Attaché) and you get one free – his wife!

The Philippines is a very hot country and so things like overhead fans are quite important. After one of our many power failures, the fan in our main sitting area was not working. We were told by the electricians that the motor was located in a space above the wooden ceiling. In order to carry out the remedial work, the entire ceiling had to be taken down to access the fan and its workings. This took two days to accomplish. I then had to write a letter to the village security department, informing them that the workmen had my permission to remove the fan from my house.

The fan was duly removed and the ceiling replaced for the duration of the repair. Several days later, the workmen returned, spent two days removing the ceiling for the second time, re-installed the fan and painstakingly replaced the wooden ceiling. The fan was switched on – and hey presto, it worked ... but only for a few minutes, after which it stopped, blowing the fuses in the whole house!

Thankfully our electrical system was restored fairly quickly. But the ceiling had to be taken down for a third time (another two days) and the fan was to be taken away for repair yet again. But first, another security clearance letter was required.

A few days later, the smiling workmen returned, and proceeded to remove the ceiling. As the fan and motor were being replaced, it slipped and crashed to the floor, narrowly missing the head of one of the electricians. Needless to say the whole procedure of the mobile ceiling was repeated.

My husband and I returned from a trip away to find that an alternative fan had been fitted in our absence. It was simply awful and totally unacceptable so it too had to be replaced. The whole saga continued for weeks.

It was one example of the frustrations of living in what one might have termed an exotic location, but really rather reflected the general inefficiency of life in the Philippines at that time.

THE MALAYSIAN JUNGLE

Have you ever been in a situation or place and thought to yourself, 'What on earth am I doing here – how did I get myself into this?' Many times no doubt, as our way of life is full of constant change. Quite a few of you reading this must have tales to tell of places where you have lived or survived.

The strangest situation I've been in was the middle of a jungle in Malaya. It was 1971. As I lay in my para-hammock I certainly wondered how … It happened like this:

At a coffee morning (of all places) one of the wives on my husband's squadron (103 Singapore) suggested that, as the men were always going off on jungle survival, why couldn't the wives do something similar?

There were shudders and shivers and 'What about the children?' Panic, panic, all trying to think of reasons why we shouldn't go. I must say I was certainly of that school of thought when the jungle trip was being discussed. We talked about it all the morning – happy days with nothing better to do. Eventually a vote was taken on who would go, or might go, and, surprisingly, we had twelve volunteers.

The Squadron Commander was approached with our suggestion

and he laughed like a drain; this, of course, made us all the more determined. He eventually realised we were serious and gave his permission, with the proviso that we had some form of training before the venture.

One hot and particularly humid morning we reported to the squadron to meet our 'teachers', who were rubbing their hands together in glee at the prospect of putting frail girls through their paces. We were kitted out with jungle boots up to, and some above, the knee on us. Flying suits were handed out which, to accommodate some of our hips, had to be several sizes too big, making us look like elephants, all baggy at the back.

Then the hats – hair being pushed up inside – some hats at an angle, some plonked on and some perched on the back of the head like sun hats. What a sight we looked, but this was no time to worry about our looks; we had to learn to survive. Then, with water bottles and machetes (huge Ghurkha-type knives) hanging from our waists, we sat ourselves down for our first lesson.

'The machete,' said the sergeant 'is the all-purpose piece of equipment.' With this we would make our bed, cut back the jungle, cut plants containing water to drink and, many of us thought, defend ourselves!

With three deft stokes into the side of a tree, lo and behold we made a ridge-type cut, around which a rope was tied securely. On the other end of the rope was a parachute. Another few cuts to the trunk of a second tree, round with the rope, pull up tight – one hammock. On with the ground sheet for our roof. It looked so easy.

When we all started hacking at our various trees the men said that our fear of tigers tearing us to pieces in the Malayan jungle would be nothing compared with what we would do to ourselves with our own machetes! A whole hour was spent on the mishandling of ours. Eventually we managed the cuts in the trees with no splinters in the eye or feet lost in the process.

After shelter came food – Compo Ration (nasty little dried biscuits), tea, sweetener, soups, even chocolate, purifying tablets for our water bottles. Giggles as we were handed our 'pills'.

Early on Saturday morning we loaded our cars and set off over the causeway from Singapore for Johore Bahru in Malaya and way beyond up the east coast. We thought it best to wear ordinary clothes through customs and don our jungle kit in some quiet place over the border. Just as well, as I feel we would have been arrested on sight! We stopped at the appointed place on the map, changed into our Action Man outfits, locked the cars and, for the rest of the morning, hacked our way about a mile into the jungle. Two men from the squadron came that far with us, but then we were on our own.

We brandished our machetes to make our camp, and sprinkled ant power around the base of the trees like cheap talc that we wanted to dispose of. We built a fire and, after numerous cups of tea and games of cards, settled down for the night.

It started to drizzle. I was in charge of thunder flashes (little explosives that, when one pulls the string and throws, go bang). We carried these to frighten off any large animals. I kept them close by – in fact too close, putting them underneath me to keep them dry before thinking, 'What if they go off?' I then wrapped them in plastic and put them a little further away.

Lying in our para-hammocks we shone our torches up into the trees, then wished we hadn't, since the trees were so tall that the beam wouldn't reach the tops and we imagined slithering, sliding, wriggling things creeping and curling around the trunk and branches. All around us we could see the lights of fire-flies, but to us they were hundreds of eyes watching and waiting.

We took it in turns to keep awake and watch the fire. At one point, glancing over in that direction, I saw the fire was almost out. I swung out of the hammock yet again, and went over to the pile of twigs that someone had thoughtfully put under a groundsheet. I tried to revive the fire by blowing into it and adding twigs. Flames at last. Then there was a slow movement from one of the hammocks nearest the fire, a head peeped over at me, a squeal and then, 'Eee, Maureen, it's you. I thought it were a wild pig!' It was our Lena from Lancashire.

'*Nelly!* Lovely of you to join us!'

Everybody was soon up again for another cup of tea. Would dawn ever come? Sitting around the fire we heard rustling noises. We looked at each other to see if anyone else had heard it. They had. Slinking slowly past we saw something spotted. A leopard?

'No, too small.'

'A baby leopard,' whispered Lena.

'No, wrong shape,' said someone.

It was about as big as next door's tom cat. It went on its way thank goodness, but none of us could go back to sleep. It was only a glimpse and no one was sure what it was, but it moved like a cat and that was enough.

By this time we were all sitting in a circle with our backs to the fire looking out. Then, quite spontaneously, we all began to sing, as so many people do in times of fear, although we didn't get as far as 'Abide with me'!

The insects knew what time it was as their noises became louder and louder. We could hear the high-pitched chatter of a distant tribe of monkeys. At last, the morning light appeared in the tree tops. Somehow, we had survived.

THE LADIES' PROGRAMME

One of the delights of a NATO HQ posting was travelling to international conferences. As those of you who have enjoyed these postings will know, a most important part of any conference was The Ladies' Programme. Each country vied to put on the best, most interesting and most immaculately planned entertainment, but none more so than the Americans – who were our hosts in Naples (Allied Forces South).

Project officers, escorts, security briefings, printed programmes – every detail was superbly planned. Nothing was to go wrong – national pride was at stake. Now it is a well-known fact that American ladies love nothing more than the opportunity for a little special shopping, hence the highlight of our day was to be a VIP tour of a factory making beautiful marble-inlay furniture. This was the reason that our large, shiny, Italian coach (complete with handsome Italian driver) was parked in the back streets of industrial Naples while we were securely escorted inside the factory.

'Please leave your possessions on the coach,' we were told. 'The driver will lock the doors and stay by the coach as guard.' Sure enough, as we emerged some time later, there was our macho Italian driver in his tight trousers and shades posing by our transport nonchalantly swinging the keys in his hand and then suddenly, horror of horrors, the keys swung out of his grip and straight down a drain in the road!

Consternation and absolute disbelief from our escorts – lots of speaking into sleeves and growing panic, HQ on max alert. This sort of rescue had not been rehearsed and any recovery plan was likely to take several hours to put into operation. It was after all, Naples in the rush hour.

How to keep us all safe and all together seemed to be the main concern. Perhaps a coffee while the panic continued? Well, coffee shops are rare in that part of Naples, but bars are plenty – deep, dark and noisy – and I think we were probably happily into our second grappa, being entertained by local factory workmen, before the next stage of the master plan was announced. The Naples local train service – a station was more or less within walking distance. Several train changes later and with a complete breakdown of security, as we were lost to sight in hot crowded carriages, we all managed to reach our destination and were met by a fleet of cars from HQ.

All ended well as the coach company returned our possessions to us later that night. But I fear our repeated reassurance to our hosts that it was a most enjoyable adventure – best bit of the programme – failed to prevent their nightmares and collective post-traumatic stress disorder.

TOO EARLY

Living in Belgium in the mid 1990s was fun, with my husband working at NATO HQ in Brussels. We had lots of parties and met some delightful people. We were sitting down to watch the TV one evening when the doorbell rang. We answered it, to find a very smart Royal Danish Air Force colonel with a beautiful bunch of flowers – having arrived exactly one week before our planned supper party. He must have thought us very relaxed about our entertaining, when we appeared in jeans and T-shirts. We invited him in, and we had a drink and a laugh, before he retired politely ready to return the following week!

LA PETITE BLONDE

In the 1960s our first posting as a young married couple was to Fontainebleau, near Paris. I, as an Australian, had not a word of French and was thrown in at the deep end, particularly when it came to shopping in the local market.

I had consulted my little dictionary and, one day, set off to buy kidneys. Unfortunately I had selected the wrong word, which refers to human kidneys. All my attempts to purchase these produced gales of laughter from both the market staff and customers, resulting in one very red-faced Australian.

Over the time of our posting it appeared that I became quite a hit with the market traders, who referred to me as '*Ma petite blonde*'!

BEETLES AND BUGS

The word 'bug' has several connotations. Bugs, for us, were nifty travel companions in the guise of mobile vehicles of some sort or another. For nostalgia's sake there were two types that featured loudly in our RAF career. In our family it was small, neat and admirably functional and the iconic 'people's car', being the first bug that endeared itself to us.

Our married life began in 1970 with ownership of a bright orange beetlebug – a Volkswagen. It was one of the first ones with a 'rectangular' back window, a departure from the oval one. How we loved that car! A true love-bug, a relationship forged not only through its being our first car but the one in which I passed my driving test. It was a very forgiving car and 'Gerry', our nickname for it, never baulked at being piled up with people, picnic paraphernalia, tents, luggage, etc – and as for parking, easy peasy! There was no other engine noise quite the same as a VW's – and such quirks as the boot being under the bonnet – how different was that?

Our love affair with Gerry was abruptly cut short when we were posted to Cyprus, land of Aphrodite and Commanderia, sun, sea and sand. Sadly we had to leave Gerry behind. However, the 'bug' had unwittingly set a standard in our psyche for ever – the slightly funky, supremely functional object of desire!

As we soon discovered, there are a few 'pet' names for the VW and much to our amazement the regular Cypriot vegetable man had a VW 'Combi' which he proudly drove round the quarters in Nicosia. He advertised his trade with panache, indeed he deserved to be cock-a-hoop. Clearly his fruit and vegetables were utterly delectable and, in his wonderful broken English, he announced, 'I'm the guy who drives the "*vax-vages*" and when you see my lovely artichokes you won't go anywhere else!' He called in every Friday morning and needed no warning as one could hear the distinguished rich, guttural engine noise well before the Combi appeared.

The second kind of bug in our lives arrived and came in the form of a red and white striped 'Chico' baby buggy, coinciding with the birth of our son in Dhekelia. The baby buggy folded down into what looked like two walking sticks with wheels, was lightweight and has to be the original work-horse. Like one of the family it came everywhere with us, never far from hand – transporting baby, changing bags, swimming things, groceries all hooked on those arm sticks. It came on buses, in cars, on boats, on beaches, in markets and then finally, in an Argosy and VC10 back to Blighty in July 1974. I clutched it fiercely, protectively, with my son in one arm and in the other hand a suitcase full of nappies as we were evacuated during the Turkish invasion.

The buggy followed us two years later, to Hong Kong – this time with a new passenger, our baby daughter. Those little wheels carried our precious cargo all over Kai Tak, Clear Water Bay Road, Stinkies (Kowloon City), La Salle Do, Worcester Heights, Yamati ferry to Hey Ling Chow Island and the rest, and this time we were joined by a beautiful pale-blue VW beetle. My, how complete did we feel! The two little toddlers tucked in the back of the 'blue bug' – no safety belts in sight – with the buggy lying in the boot, careering all over the city, New Territories, going to school, visiting friends on the Peak, picnics on junks, and the traffic! 'Mojo', the name we had for the beetle, scurried into spaces that you only dream of in front of taxis (the main protagonists), past pushy cars, buses and trolley buses and never once came a cropper. What a star!

And so the buggy story continued – same one, but this time to Kuwait carrying son number two. It had become part of the family, after all, like a trusty nanny you never let go! The miles those little wheels turned and never once did it let us down. It acted as prop when the mother-of-three had no hands left – steering through crowded streets, little hands clutching tightly to those itinerant walking-stick handles, and bags of baby detritus slung over them. It was a comfort to the tired little body often seen sleeping in the semi-propped up position, seemingly impossibly uncomfortable but, oh, what relief there was!

Where would we be without the use of those beetles and buggies? They went hand in hand with our life overseas – enhancing our lives immeasurably. How did we fit all that stuff into the beetlebug and travel to all those places with the buggy? The colourful tapestry of our lives, lived in those far-off countries, could only have been enhanced by such ownership. I think the simplicity of the bugs has to be the nub – the memory of them stays loud and clear to this day as we cream along in the Polo and wrestle with the newfangled, grandchildren's 'baby-transporters'!

INTRUDERS

I lived in Singapore in the 1960s, accompanying my husband who was with the helicopter force, on 103 Squadron. With no children and few 'points' in order to be entitled to live in a married quarter, we had to find private rented accommodation. We found a semi-detached house off the Thompson Road near the McRitchie Reservoir. My husband was away a lot of time, either in Hong Kong, or on exercise in Malaya. I acquired a dog called Charlie Brown, a sheepdog cross Labrador. The house had frosted windows and bars across every window, as well as an iron sliding-railing type door on the front patio, again with frosted glass in between. The problem with not being able to see out, with all the doors and windows locked at night and just the fan whizzing around on the ceiling (no aircon in those days), was that one could imagine all kinds of things that were going on outside, being on the edge of jungle as it was in those days.

One night I was woken by loud shouts and banging. Charlie Brown was barking and all the hairs on his neck were standing on end. Charlie and I came downstairs, me clutching my nightie about my throat (I find I still do this in times of fear!). We were afraid. It seemed that someone or several people were banging on the bars of my front window. I was not going to open the door or even a window. Telephone – I rushed to the telephone, it was still 999 then, and I told the police that a gang was trying to break into my house. Charlie and I waited and still the bars on the window in the front were vibrating. I thought, they will be in my house in a minute.

Then, silence, no shouting, no banging but the noise of a Land Rover. I then had the courage to peep out of the window and saw the Singapore police. They were laughing, but looking towards my neighbour's house. At that point I had the courage to open the door and railings, and I saw my neighbour Mr Yo looking over my fence and holding something. The police said, 'Missie, you call police?'

'Yes,' I said, 'but where are all the people?'

Mr Yo laughed and laughed with the police and held up an enormous dead snake for me to see. What had happened was, the snake had wound itself around the bars of his window, that was attached to mine, and he was beating the snake to death on the bars, in so doing vibrating the railings on my windows.

I asked the police, 'That snake, it bite, it kill?' and they said, 'No Missie, it strangle.' It was a 15-foot boa constrictor! Silly me.

RUMBLE IN THE NIGHT

It was the early 1980s and our first night in our new 'temporary' home in Berlin. I was just drifting off to sleep when I became aware of a curious droning noise. I listened intently; had I turned off the TV? Was the central heating okay? I sat up and listened again to be sure I wasn't imagining it. No, I wasn't, and it was getting louder. I shook my husband awake, which took some time, saying, 'There's a strange noise, wake up! Wake up! Can you hear that rumble? It's getting louder.'

Slowly he pushed himself up onto his elbows and listened. After a moment's hesitation I knew he could hear it too. He sat up and looked at his watch. It was only two in the morning and the source of the noise was getting ever closer. It was clear it was coming from outside. We went over to the patio doors, stepped out onto the balcony and looked down Kaiserdamm.

'Oh my God!' we both whispered and clutched at each other in fear for, as far as we could see, tanks were rolling in from the direction of East Berlin! It was beginning to snow, so the air was slightly murky, which made the scene all the more sinister.

'Of all the days the Russians could have chosen to invade, it's the day WE arrive in Berlin, bloody typical!' I said, then speaking in lower tones, 'We've got to get the children out!'

We had both been watching in horror for several moments when my husband turned slowly to look at me. He was smiling. 'It's not the Russians, look, it's the Americans. They must be on manoeuvres!'

I looked down on to the leading tank and there, sure enough, was the American white star emblazoned on its turret. We hugged each other and danced around the balcony.

Typical of the American forces, there was a GI riding atop the turret of every tank. We leaned over the balcony and waved to them excitedly. The American forces obviously loved to be appreciated and acknowledged us as they passed. This is what it must have felt like at the liberation of Paris!

What must the Americans have thought at the sight of two people waving at them so enthusiastically at two in the morning! They probably thought we were drunk! But what a sight. As we watched the tanks thundering past I thought of all the times in recent history that the Berliners must have watched just such a scene and been just as terrified as we were moments before. I hoped that I would never have to experience anything like it. It made me realise what an important role the Allied Occupation of West Berlin played in this game called the Cold War, if it was keeping freedom alive.

THE GOLD SOUK

Many years ago we were posted to Saudi Arabia, and on day two I had to find my way to the Souk to buy sheets and towels as well as food in order to allow us to entertain a group of RAF officers from London. Later that day my husband and I took our visitors to the Gold Souk. As a woman I was wearing the necessary Abiyah – a long black coat – but did not possess the regulation scarf since our luggage was still en route from the UK. One minute I was in the company of this jolly band of officers, and then they vanished in a puff of smoke.

The reason was that they had spotted the approach of a Mutawah, a religious policeman and, knowing the local scene better than I, wanted to see the reaction. The Mutawah proceeded to tick me off for being improperly dressed. Where were my gallant husband and his colleagues – all laughing around the corner! This was perhaps not the best introduction to a new tour, although I have to admit that the Mutawah were generally polite and courteous to me.

HASSAN

It was November 1970 and I was 18 years old. I had been married for six weeks, and was living with my husband, a flying officer, in

Manama, Bahrain. We had a small, rather shabby little apartment with a sort of 1960s metal-framed, French window style front door. It had a broken lock, and had to be kept shut with the use of a broom handle. One of the panes of glass had been replaced by a piece of brown chipboard with a large hole in the middle, and number 48 painted in white on the outside. We didn't live at number 48.

Whenever anything needed fixing, Hassan would turn up. He was a delightful, wiry old man, with a crumpled brown face and rather grubby clothes. Hassan's accomplishments would fill up a book on their own, but I do remember some well. For example, there was the window pane he replaced with the putty on the inside of the left half, and on the outside of the right, leaving it at a permanently jaunty angle. The time he painted the bathroom walls and left two large spaces unpainted where the ladder had rested. He changed the lock on the front door – three days of work later, I was proudly shown the finished result. We now had a locking door, with a handle on one side and a spindle through the door that was four inches too long, the square edges of which had been filed down to fit the round hole in the handle which, in turn, was held in place with a bent nail. I said it was perfect.

However, his *pièce de résistance* was when he came to fix the water heater. It was a large, probably 10-gallon, tank which was situated directly over a huge and somewhat rusty fridge. He clambered nimbly up onto the top of the fridge taking my small washing-up bowl with him. I started to say, 'Hassan you're not going to …' but was interrupted by a raised hand and 'Memsahib, Hassan will do it!' At this point he undid the bottom of the tank and the aforementioned 10 gallons of water gushed out and, obviously not contained by the washing-up bowl, flooded the kitchen and most of the hall. He gave me an 'If Allah wills it, what can Hassan do', sort of look, removed his headdress, and proceeded to mop up the water with it.

At this point I went out, shutting the door with the wonky handle and the chipboard panel with the hole and the number 48 painted in white, and left for the souk.

SPRECHEN SIE DEUTSCH?

We were thrilled about our posting to 92 Squadron in RAF Germany in the late 1960s where my husband would be flying Lightnings on his first operational squadron. We packed up our home at RAF Coltishall in Norfolk and drove to Dover to get the ferry to Zeebrugge. This was extremely exciting for us because

RAF Valley in Wales was the nearest we had ever come to living any of our married life abroad so, when we docked in Zeebrugge, we were driving on the Continent for the very first time.

After a very lengthy road journey, on appalling autobahns in those days, we arrived at our new flat in Annenstrasse in the small town of Gutersloh, not far from the Miele washing machine factory. Little did we realise in those early days just how long it was going to take for a poor flying officer and his wife, with no marriage allowance and no married quarter because we were considered too young to be married, to be able to afford a Miele.

On arrival at the flat we were both starving, and because the shops had closed by the time we arrived we decided that we would have to find a Bratwurst stall, the equivalent of a UK fish and chip shop. With only a smattering of schoolboy German between us we started practising how to ask for 'chicken and chips for two'. We decided *'Zweimal halbes Hanchen mit Pommes Frittes und Mayonnaise bitte'*, would fit the bill and we giggled our way to the 'Bratty Stall' at the end of our road.

We queued nervously with the local Germans until it was our turn to order and my husband started confidently as we had planned, *'Guten Abend, Zweimal halbes Hanchen mit Pommes Frittes und Mayonnaise bitte'*, whereupon the friendly lady behind the counter said, 'D'yer wannem wrapped or yer gonna eat 'em 'ere?'

This spoilt the atmosphere somewhat, but we laughed a lot that night – our very first night together on our first overseas squadron tour.

AN EMPTY GLASS

We were at Ramstein Air Base in Germany, where my husband was serving on the staff of AIRCENT, a major NATO headquarters. At the time, there were six nations represented in the headquarters and, in addition to having a full-on social life among the British contingent, we mixed as much as possible with the officers and wives from all the other nations. Indeed, an important aspect of working in such a multi-national environment was to get to know how the other nations operated and to learn as much about their cultures as possible.

We had made friends with a German couple who had invited us to dinner one evening. Everything was going very well and, in typical German fashion, nothing had been left to chance. We found an immaculate table setting, delightful flower arrangements, perfect food, beautifully chilled German wine, and easygoing conversation. The conversation was very relaxed and interesting as our hosts described, in some detail, a house they still owned in the middle of Berlin. It transpired that they had not seen it for over 30 years, while the Berlin Wall was in place, and that now developers were offering them vast sums of money for it.

However, while this enthralling tale was being told, my husband and I were sipping our wine with ever-reducing sips. Our hosts on the other hand kept re-filling their own glasses with gay abandon. We therefore took even smaller sips in order not to empty our glasses, while our hosts continued to fill theirs, even opening another bottle to do so. When our glasses became so low that another sip became impossible, our host eventually asked why we did not enjoy the wine, which was one of his favourites. I explained that we liked it very much and would love some more.

'Oh,' he explained, 'in Germany it is the custom not to re-fill a person's wine glass until it is completely empty.'

'Oh,' I replied, 'in the UK it is our custom to keep a person's wine glass topped up so that it never becomes empty.'

We laughed loudly and the evening progressed in fine form as we were indulged with copious quantities of the most excellent German wine. The moral of the tale – beware cultural differences.

6

On Parade and in a Mess

A PAT ON THE BOTTOM

Having cats, predominantly white furry ones, inevitably means that furniture gets covered in fine hair. Prior to the AOC's (a very senior officer) arrival for a dining-in night, I had (I thought) de-animalised the lounge thoroughly. However as the men, dressed in their mess kits, were about to leave after their hastily consumed G&Ts, I was horrified to notice that our senior guest had a significant collection of white cat's hair all over his bottom.

Taking a deep breath (this was not a person I knew very well), I reappeared with the clothes brush and, having sought his permission, proceeded to attack with vigour said VIP bum before giving him the all-clear to go! My husband was not impressed – but I wonder how often he had appeared at dining-in nights with a 'hairy' bum that I hadn't checked!

WRONG SHOES

While halfway through the drive to an Annual Formal Inspection of one of hubby's stations, I looked down at my feet and realised I had different shoes on, one blue and one black! Fortunately our driver knew some girls (lots, in fact) and, having dropped us off, he disappeared, returning in short time with a matching pair – and in my size.

FIRE FIRE!

It was a hot summer's day at a small RAF base in eastern England. Occasion: the Annual Formal Inspection or AFI visit. I had been invited for lunch by Mrs Station Commander to meet Mrs Air Marshal. My son, home on a weekend exeat, had asked earlier if he could make himself a picnic and eat it near the airfield. 'Why ever not,' I thought and duly agreed.

While enjoying the pre-drinks and chat before we sat down, the Station Commander's steward suddenly appeared and said my son was at the front door and anxious to see me. Slightly irritated, I went to where my son was hopping from foot to foot. He informed me that he thought I should know there was a small fire on the airfield. Noticing his grubby face and singed appearance, I told the steward I hoped to be back soon and dragged said son across to the edge of the married patch where the airfield began. It wasn't far, but tricky in high-heeled white sandals (so 'in' that year!), to where a small fire had taken hold in the very dry grass.

Hastening home with chastened son in tow, I rang the fire section and said there was a small fire on the airfield and asked them not to make a big issue of it because of the AFI visit.

Inevitably the men had just sat down to lunch in the Mess when over the tannoy came, 'FIRE, FIRE, Fire on the airfield!' So much for keeping it low-key. Apparently the Station Commander looked slightly surprised but the Air Marshal thought it was all part of the day's scenario and was very impressed by the quick reaction and timing.

I returned to a very pleasant lunch while our son ate the charred remains of his picnic in our garden.

MANNERS

We were often asked to official functions off-base, and so it was that one evening we travelled to Wrexham, my husband to attend a guest night at an army mess, while the ladies were to have supper with the Colonel's wife. Having arrived at the gate to her house, I was just wondering how to get into it when a very loud plummy voice in my ear boomed, 'This way, follow me!' Having introduced myself and explained how I came to be there, my fellow-guest thrust her hand at me, told me her name and departed to 'circulate' without another word.

About a week later we were invited to have Sunday lunch with a delightful couple who were well known and down-to-earth local landowners. We happened to arrive at about the same time as the aforementioned lady, accompanied by her husband, who was clad in one of those orange hairy tweed suits. The Voice boomed out, 'Good lord, it's you again!' As we sipped pre-lunch drinks, she came over to me and said, 'You haven't met my husband yet. Henry, this is … what did you say your name was?' Any affront I might have felt was dispelled by the sight of this poor man's flies – not that I was deliberately looking in that direction, you understand. Anyway, the zip had obviously broken at some stage, and The Voice had replaced it without a gusset!

Sixteen of us went into the dining room and I was seated to the left of our host. The Voice was seated two up from me, with another very pleasant landowner between us. The starter was salmon, caught by the host himself. We were chatting away at the end of this course when the hostess called to her husband to come and carve the roast. We hadn't really had time to deal with the plates from the first course, so I started by putting the host's plate on top of mine. The Voice immediately boomed out, 'Good God, you're not stacking, are you?' to which I replied, 'Well, the plates were empty, and I wasn't scraping.'

By this time most of the assembled company was listening. The Voice turned to the gentleman seated between us, and said, 'Reminds me of a little anecdote I once heard; are you aristocracy, or do you stack?'

What could I say? My response was simply, 'Although clearly I am not aristocracy, I have been taught some manners!' The barely-suppressed – in fact, not suppressed at all – mirth from around the table suggested that perhaps I had won the encounter on points.

HOSTING THE US GENERAL

RAF Binbrook, a Lightning Air Defence station in a remote part of the Lincolnshire Wolds, was chosen as a venue for an Anglo/US conference. The Station was asked to host the delegates, and volunteers were needed to provide overnight accommodation for the many US generals flying in. As an encouragement we were even each offered a steward to press the visitor's mess kit and help with breakfast!

We lived in one of the rather splendid old Lutyens houses – totally unmodernised at the time – a multitude of elegant bedrooms and one small bathroom. It was freezing cold and icy winds straight from the Urals rattled the old sash windows. This was also the 1970s – the time of the 'winter of discontent', the three-day week, miners' strikes, frequent power cuts and fuel shortages.

'Our' general was straight out of 'central casting' – short hair, chiselled jaw, lean and gung-ho and dressed in an immaculate lightweight uniform, so sharp it looked as though it would never need pressing. He liked to go for an early morning run or visit the gym, I was informed! Well I wasn't quite sure whether the station had the sort of gym he would be used to – and, looking out of the window at the dank Binbrook weather, and hearing the musical whine of the bitter wind blowing through the letter box, I wasn't sure about the early morning run either.

However, we had all made a big effort and hoped he would be very comfortable. First visit to Europe he told me – just flown in from Texas – bit confused by the time change, definitely failed to be briefed about the weather and obviously unaware of the current British political situation. As he went to change into mess kit for the formal dinner we had a power cut. I tried to explain about three-day weeks and miners' strikes as I lit the emergency candles, but I could see disbelief creeping in. Actually he managed rather well by candlelight and was driven off to the Mess where thankfully generators were running. However, coming back in the dark he obviously mistook the bed I had turned down – the one with the freshly starched sheets and warm fleecy blankets, and slept in the twin bed – the one the cats considered their own, the one with the little nest in the pillows covered with cat hairs.

The next day there was no sign of the early morning run. The winter morning was dark and jet lag had really taken its hold, but I was heartened that breakfast seemed to be going rather well. That was until one of the cats – now in full hostess mode – brought in a gift of a live mouse which, for the rest of his stay, ran round the house watched by a dog and two cats.

I didn't see our general again – he flew back to Texas immediately after the conference as fast as he could. I wonder what stories he told – 'It's like the Middle Ages over there – they live in freezing, old-fashioned, mice-ridden quarters with no electricity!'

OPEN DAY AT ODIHAM

As usual at our annual Open Day at RAF Odiham I, as a junior officer's wife, helped on the cake stall. On this particular occasion the walnut trees around the camp were in full fruit, so we decided to collect the nuts and sell them with the cakes.

We did well and sold out. One of our senior officers' wives bought a large bag of them but, as she was to accompany the Mayor of Basingstoke on her helicopter trip home, I offered to drop them off at her house once the Open Day was over. After we had cleared up, I walked there, pushing my young son in his pram and, as she had not yet returned, I left the bag on her front door step.

Thinking nothing more of it, I returned home and started to prepare the evening meal. When my husband returned, he told me that there had been an incident on that part of the married patch that housed the senior officers' families.

It transpired that the package on the doorstep had appeared suspicious to her husband on his return home. He had called the bomb disposal boys in to have a look at it, but before they did so, all the neighbouring families had had to leave their houses. You can imagine the outcome when the bag was found to contain walnuts. Was my face red!!!

FRIDAY EVENINGS

Ye've a' heard Tam O'Shanter's tale
Of Rabbie's liking for the ale
A common failing o' the male
I'm here tae tell ye

He loved the lassies, so we're told
And chased them a', whe'er young or old
I doubt if he'd hae been sae bold
If he'd e'er been sober

But are ye menfolk a' the same
And chant ye all the same refrain?
'A woman's place is in the hame
While we're oot drinkin''

There's one breed that I know quite well
They pride themsel's on raisin' hell
So lend yer ears, a tale I'll tell
O' fighter pilots

Despite the skill that they display
They're normal folk, or so they say
But once a week they gang astray
It's on a Friday evening

ON PARADE AND IN A MESS

The Bosses lead them by the nose
And tak them where the drinkie flows
Tae tell tall stories, or just pose
Every Friday evening

They go on trips tae distant lands
And leave the lassies in a band
Wi' golf and bridge and tea in hand
Tae cope wi' lonely evenings

The hamecomin' will be the same
The trip was hard, but they're no tae blame
They'll dump the kit, mess up the hame
And no' a word a' evenin'

Then doon the bothy, can't be late
Tae drink a toast and celebrate
That they can still participate
In yet mare Friday evenings

Dinny gang, it's no yet time
Tae face the nagger's endless whine,
'Where ha'e ye been, ye drunken swine?
Yer meal's in the dug this evening'

Whit mischief dae they plan tae hatch?
There must be somewhere on the patch
A friendly door left on the latch
Fer eggie-bakes this evenin'

So noo it's time tae heed fer hame
Tae face the sullen sulky dame
Who's waiting for someone tae maim
Fer ruining her evenin'

But wait, his open bedroom door
And the smilin' lass that he adores
Whit a pity he can only snore
Ever Friday evenin'

ARMY BEDS

Between postings in the mid 1990s, my 'one-star' husband spent three months on an intensive course at the Army Staff College at Camberley. He was comfortably installed in a huge bedroom, 'big as a ballroom', where a lorry load of textbooks and a laptop were provided.

Towards the end of the course, the wives were invited to a special dinner and this gave me the opportunity to see the accommodation in which my husband had been holed up for so long. As there was only one standard single bed, he arranged for an additional bed to be brought in so that I could stay the night.

The college itself is a lovely building and, as expected, the interior was as formidably grand as any military establishment. Imagine my shock on entering my husband's room. Sparse was an understatement. A desk, chair and a bed crowded into a huge space! A second single bed had duly been delivered and set up as far away as was possible from my husband's retreat. In fact it was a good 10 paces away across the room!

I have coped with many unenviable situations during our thirty odd years together, but my sense of humour almost deserted me when I then discovered I had to walk along a lengthy, draughty corridor, down a flight of steps and along another corridor to reach the ladies' bathroom!

A CLOSE SHAVE

We were raising money for charity – weren't we always! Someone had the bright idea that people might pay for the pleasure of removing someone else's hair ... from the upper lip, the eyebrows, the scalp even – but only with their agreement, of course.

I had arrived at the Mess rather later than usual, but obviously there had been, and still were, great goings on. I was just in time to see our padre, a large gregarious Irishman, making his way to the door, moustache still intact. I would never have put him down as a bad sport; not the chap who rode a Harley (with Harleylujah! on the number plate) and wore a biking jacket with 'Vicar' emblazoned in studs on the back. He was also the bass player in the rock band.

I did try to persuade him to join in the fun and part with his moustache but he said he would have to kill anyone who despoiled his pride and joy! Having haggled for a while, he eventually agreed to let me shave his chest, for the vast sum of £10. So we went back into the bar, where I was provided with the necessary tools. The victim unbuttoned his shirt; he did indeed have a very hairy chest. I told him not to worry because I was used to cutting my husband's hair and there would be not so much as a nick; he was just to look away and think of England – or, in his case, Ireland.

It took a little while to complete the work of art and, with the help of some black boot polish, I was able to make the hair even darker and thus the pattern even clearer. It was a large inverted V with an S in the middle, because we all thought of him as 'Superman' anyway.

When he saw the results of my efforts in the mirror, he became quite agitated and said that his wife would certainly have something to say about it. I said I would happily launder the sheets but he said that the boot polish wasn't the problem because he could have a shower before he went to bed. The real problem was that he was taking his family abroad on holiday the next day!

WHERE ARE THEY?

We were on our first tour in Germany in the late 1960s and my husband had the lowly duty of Squadron Entertainment Officer, a task always given to the junior pilot on a squadron. On this particular weekend he had organised a party in the crewroom. Squadron parties in those days were wild events. We worked hard, we partied hard, we were young, there was no such thing as drink-driving, and we could keep going well into the small hours. Crewroom parties were particularly energetic events because the ambience of a crewroom was fairly basic, there was little chance of causing any permanent damage, and they were far enough away from anything resembling civilisation that noise was never an issue. The aftermath of these parties however was dire, and it usually took an army of willing volunteers to clear up the mess.

However, showing the potential of someone who hoped one day to rise to the dizzy heights of a senior officer in the RAF, my husband had on this occasion decided to impress his bosses and fellow squadron pilots by not asking them to help clear up. Instead he had arranged with Willi, our very German Mess Manager, to replace this usual army of willing volunteers with an altogether more professional bunch of clearers-up, namely the Italian staff of the Officers' Mess. It had been agreed with Willi that they would turn up at the squadron crewroom the following morning to put everything back to normal.

My husband and I arrived in good time that morning to oversee the Italian contingent, collected the keys from the guardroom, opened up the crewroom, and waited. The appointed hour came and went, we gave them a little more time, but eventually with no sign of our Italian brethren my husband phoned Willi in the Officers' Mess to ask what had happened to them. I remember the conversation clearly.

My husband said, 'Willi, where are the Italians? I can't find them anywhere.'

To which Willi replied, 'Sir, vee have ze same problem in ze last vor.'

Who says Germans don't have a sense of humour!

STAFF COURSE REVUE

The 1982 Staff Course at RAF Bracknell was nearly at an end. The men had completed their lectures and papers, the Brooke-Popham essays had been delivered and the wives had survived the non-stop social scene. New postings and promotions had been received, the removal companies were called and we were winding down.

Some gallant souls, both husbands and wives, had offered themselves up for the much anticipated End of Course Revue. It would inevitably involve a lot of comic sketches and the directing staff were probably eagerly and nervously looking forward to their students letting their hair down! Neither my husband nor I was bold enough to take part and, on the night, we joined the large audience who were already clapping and cheering anything that appeared to move behind the closed stage curtains. It was a brilliant show, almost a pantomime!

Quite suddenly, the curtains opened for the next turn and, at centre stage, was a lectern. There was a definite hush, then a tall imposing RAF officer in informal 'woolly pully' kit strode on, notes in hand.

'Good evening ladies and Gentlemen, I want to …' An audible groan was heard as a telephone rang loudly. The officer looked sideways, then at the audience, and said, 'Excuse me,' and disappeared off stage. But in a matter of seconds he returned glancing at his notes. 'Good evening, again …'

Funny, I could have sworn that it had been an Air Force officer not an Army officer. My thoughts were interrupted by the sound of the phone again, and the officer looking peeved muttered, 'I'm so sorry.'

There was an atmosphere brewing in the theatre – you could feel it. In a nanosecond the RAF chap was back on stage being terribly apologetic.

By now I was confused – and looking around, I was not the only one. So our 'lecturer' had the dubious distinction of changing clothes at the speed of sound – that was it! I began to scrutinise his shoes and trousers, yes, shiny black and Air Force blue.

Then the phone shrilled again. The audience were getting into the swing of it as our man in blue side-stepped off stage. Before you could blink, he was back at the lectern, wearing a brown 'woolly pully', khaki trousers and brown shoes. This nonchalant officer was coming back and forth in alternate uniform, all the while po-faced and attempting to deliver his lecture.

By now the audience were in tears, shrieking with laughter and a slow handclap had begun.

All was eventually revealed. Our RAF officer had an identical twin brother who happened to be on the directing staff of the Army Staff Course at Camberley! They were like two peas in a pod and grinning from ear to ear!

A RETURN VISIT

Since leaving the RAF we have enjoyed returning to the fold for many special events and anniversaries. A few years ago, revisiting a Scottish Station for a squadron reunion, we were booked into the Officers' Mess.

The manager politely escorted us to the VIP suite where we were assailed by a howling gale from open windows and a strange over-whelming smell – a cross between wet paint, sickly air freshener and, could it be rotten fish? After apologising for any 'slight smell' we might notice the manager also pointed out that we might find the bathroom carpet rather wet underfoot – in fact, would we mind not using the bath, there was another bathroom down the corridor.

Much later, in the bar, I heard the full story. A visit from a former CAS prompted a last minute look at the VIP accommodation – really, the dreadful old bathroom needed an update – perhaps they could run to a new bath. One thing led to another – a hastily installed bath led to a major plumbing leak which led to a new carpet laid on still sodden floors – stuck down with fish glue – which led to the need for a little fresh paint – which led to radiators full on to speed drying – which warmed up the damp fish glue. Cue several tins of air freshener and open windows. Perhaps they won't notice! Personally I would have been very happy with the old familiar suite with perhaps the luxury of a soft pillow.

This story reminded me of the return of Terry Waite from captivity. He was initially accommodated in the Officers' Mess at RAF Brize Norton. Somehow, the *Daily Mail* was able to photograph his room and publish it under the heading 'This suite is what only the RAF could call VIP'. I'm sure Terry Waite thought it was luxury!

SINGLE ROOMS

It was in the mid 1970s that my husband, then Squadron Leader and CO of a University Air Squadron, told me with a big grin on his face that we would both be going to Cranwell for the weekend. It was the annual UAS conference; wives were invited and there would be a special programme for them. He was looking forward to the event; not only would there be many old friends with whom to compare notes but, as an 'Old Cranwellian', he would enjoy being at the college again.

The briefing notes arrived, informing us that our accommodation was reserved in the Junior Ranks Mess, Block 79. 'Home from home,' smiled my beloved, relishing the prospect. All those memories of mischief in the college and zooming above it in his Jet Provost! He had spent almost three years there as a cadet, and could cheerfully reminisce for hours.

The commanding officers and their wives would travel from as far afield as Edinburgh and Exeter and many locations between, while we drove from Liverpool. Everyone arrived on cue, eager to dump the luggage in their rooms and gather in the bar for a good gossip and a beer. Our room numbers were already allotted – it was certainly well organised and even sounded luxurious – two rooms per couple. Surely not suites?

The duty NCO announced that the officers were to take the single rooms upstairs on the first floor, while the wives were allocated bedrooms on the ground floor. He was having us on, surely? But no, each room was designed for sole occupation.

An Air Force *'fait accompli'*! There was nothing we could do, unless we were prepared to sneak up or down stairs during the night to sandwich ourselves into a single bed. Just to cap it all, some clever dick had cunningly placed each man exactly above the room of his wife below!

COLD WAR COCKTAILS

The early 1970s found us at the Joint Headquarters in Rheindahlen. It was an exceptionally busy tour socially as my husband was an ADC. I managed to keep up in spite of caring for two children at the time, aged 1 and 2. I paid my baby sitter a monthly 'wage' as she spent many nights staying in our house and even travelled away with us at times.

One interesting invitation was to a cocktail party at the Russian compound or Soviet Mission, known as Soxmiss. We would travel with my husband's boss and wife, together with the PSO and his wife. An Andover aircraft would fly us to Gutersloh and then we would transfer to a helicopter for the short flight to an unidentified (to me) location.

Being the ADC, my husband's job was to organise the cars to Wildenrath followed by the air travel. My job was the tricky one. Finding someone to look after the two little ones from three o'clock in the afternoon, feed them and put them to bed, until about 9.30 pm or later. Luckily, the PSO's wife had a live-in nanny to look after her little boy and, although she didn't drive, she agreed to take on the task. It was not so easy, as our respective quarters were some distance apart and only one of the children was old enough to walk!

We worked it all out. I would drop my two off at the other

quarter in Marlborough Road at 3 pm, come home, prepare the food for the children's teatime when the nanny would bring them to our house in Forfar Way. She would bath and change nappies, etc and put our two children to bed, then wait for the baby sitter to take over at 6.30 pm for the evening. She'd then walk back to Marlborough Road and put her own charge to bed.

I had never left my children with anyone else at this stage, so I was rather nervous about it all. The nanny was lovely but quite aged and I worried that she would find keeping three children between the age of 1 and 3 too daunting.

The day came and I delivered the kids. No problem. I returned home to metamorphose into evening attire to complement the mess kit and aiguillettes which were laid out for my husband.

It was all rather glamorous and exciting, flying off to a cocktail party hosted by Russians! I half expected James Bond to parachute in and share a glass of vodka with us. Nevertheless, at the back of my mind were the images of two little faces.

Everything went according to plan and with gifts of fine bottles of vodka, we returned to Gutersloh by helicopter, where the Andover was all warmed up ready to whisk us back to Wildenrath. I felt perfectly relaxed by this stage. There had been no SOS calls from Rheindahlen. At last we got home to find a smiling babysitter and the little cherubs fast asleep. What an adventure.

It wasn't until the next day that I discovered that, in spite of my meticulous planning for all contingencies, I had forgotten to give the front door key to the nanny. A neighbour had rescued the stressed lady, found a ladder and managed to get into the house through the bathroom window. The babysitter had been unaware of the drama and I guessed that the poor nanny had fled back home to Marlborough Road.

SUBLIME TO THE RIDICULOUS

There was nothing quite like the experience of living 'on base' of a major headquarters, and back in the 1970s, the Joint Headquarters at Rheindahlen provided all the pomp, ceremony and excitement of a multinational lifestyle. Colourful parades welcomed the many senior visiting dignitaries, both political and military, while the two officers' messes were always kept on their toes with huge formal dinners complemented by glittering military brass bands.

As the wife of a junior RAF officer, I thought the Ladies' Guest Nights were well worth the cost of a new frock, to be able to dress to the nines and enjoy dining in sumptuous surroundings. The tables would be stunningly decorated with silver candelabra, dripping with fragrant flowers bought from the flower markets over the border in Holland. The mess stewards would be immaculate as they served our dinner with military timing and precision and our glasses would be constantly replenished with delicious German wines.

Following the meal would be the speeches and, inevitably, the formal toasts. For every distinguished guest present, his or her Head of State would be toasted. This meant a Michael Bentine list of difficult names and appointments, resulting in numerous guests struggling to keep straight faces.

I would often recall these amusing details as my mind wandered during many of my husband's subsequent speeches as CO of a University Air Squadron. He had been posted to Liverpool as the new boss and, it was a far cry from Rheindahlen. The mess was an old Nissen hut, but at night its whole floor-space could be transformed into an elegant dining room.

As our first Ladies Guest Night approached I was invited to discuss the menu with our civilian mess manager, and I brought up the subject of the tables, flowers and candelabra, etc. I was not to worry, he assured me. He and his staff were well used to decorating the tables and there really was nothing for me to do.

I chose one of my favourite dresses for the occasion and my beloved was resplendent in his RAF Mess Kit. The flying instructors, students, their girlfriends and selected guests were standing at the places in the dining room as we entered. My face must have been a picture as we walked to the top table. I couldn't believe my eyes. It was the variety and mix of colour which grasped my attention first. Then it was the paper doilies, on which stood plastic flower pots containing plastic chrysanthemums. I had no idea that they came in so many shades! There was no Mess Silver, but the arrangements were beautifully lined up with military precision!

7

Husbands and Other Animals

RAILWAY SLEEPER

Now I would be the first to admit that the motion of a train at the end of a hard day's work might have a soporific effect. Add a beer (or two, or more) to the equation, and you have the potential for an unscheduled arrival at an unplanned destination and an irate spouse who, it is anticipated, will become a midnight taxi driver (or retrieval operative)!

The first occasion happened in the days before mobile phones. Following a call from King's Cross announcing the proposed arrival time home, said husband did not arrive and so I had a mild panic. My father wisely stated, 'He'll turn up,' and another call came at 0100 reporting my errant spouse to have overshot Huntingdon station and to be in York. He finally got home at 0400 and I (foolishly) thought it a 'one-off'.

Oh no – this was merely the start of a criss-crossing of southern England over the following years. My man has ended up (among other places) at:

- Didcot (Where? I had to get the road atlas out at midnight for the recovery from there and was greeted when I arrived by a BR official who asked 'Have you come from Maidenhead? I'll go and get him'!)
- Stroud (How on earth did you get there?)
- Bath (No. I am NOT going to drive two hours at midnight

to collect you and then bring you home. I'm working tomorrow!)

- Ash (No. Do not wander away from this remote station in the middle of nowhere or I will never find you.)
- Richmond, Surrey (Hello dear. The car hooting its horn is me! Stop wandering in and out of dodgy night clubs trying to get them to let you re-charge your mobile phone. Yes that's me you're looking towards, out of the car now and screaming at you to attract your attention!)
- Guildford (How am I expected to know that there are stations on both sides of the main line and that obviously you would be at the other one?)
- Staines (No. I am not coming to collect you. If you cross over the bridge and wait for 20 minutes there will be another train coming that will bring you home again.)
- Paddington (You've 'lost' your briefcase and your ticket? So who gave you the money for the fish and chips you were eating when your son and I arrived from the Shires to collect you?)

And then there was the occasion I really caused a stir. It is my habit to stay in the car when meeting the appointed train and wait for my husband to find me. On this day, intuition (or perhaps the accurate evaluation of the amount of alcohol that had been consumed) told me that he would definitely be asleep when he reached the station. As usual he had not answered his mobile two minutes before the train arrived, so I made an exception.

As the train pulled in, I started walking the length of the platform, looking in all the carriages. The guard spotted me and asked the problem: I replied that I suspected my husband would be asleep on his train and he responded that he would hold up its departure. I was now running the length of the (long) train and found him, slumped fast asleep and snoring, in a fairly full carriage.

Alerting the guard to the fact that I had located him, this screaming banshee then rushed into the carriage, grabbed husband by the lapels and shrieked at him to wake up. I grabbed the Blackberry lying on the seat vibrating to itself, and bundled him off the train, waving my thanks to the guard.

As we made a less than 'dignified' exit from the platform, husband bouncing off the railings, we passed the stationmaster who smiled benignly and said, 'Off home for a black coffee, are we?'

NOT JUST ANY DOG

Everyone else was having babies so, instead, we had a yellow Labrador pup named 'Kate', after the newest baby in the 'Archers'. She followed the flag like a good dutiful family member and provided us with numerous happy memories.

At Cranwell, aged 6 months, she delighted in slipping her leash in the environs of the parade square so she could dash in and out of the blue trouser-clad legs that were practising their marching. I, meanwhile, hid in the large rhododendron bushes at the side of the square and tried in vain to coax her back. She never did find her master's legs and I had no alternative but to come out of hiding and, with very red face, retrieve her.

By the time she was a year old we had moved to Leuchars where she loved the beaches and the open spaces. But on more than several occasions she chased rabbits under the fence and onto the airfield and was then completely out of bounds and beyond my reach. Air Traffic Control were quick to respond, sending a Land Rover to pick up the intruder who proudly sat in the front seat looking more like a celebrity than a threat, as she was chauffeured back to the guard room. I meanwhile cycled home to await the inevitable phone call instructing me to collect the wayward beast and again suffer the embarrassment of a lecture. She became quite well known, our name clearly emblazoned on her collar, but never once did anyone contact my husband!

We moved to Cottesmore, bought our first house in the village and, needless to say, were on a very tight budget. On Christmas Eve

afternoon, as we walked past the village pub, Kate disappeared and came back carrying an enormous ham joint, so big she could hardly lift it. I was mortified. My first thought was how are we going to pay for this? I carefully removed it from her and, having secured her on a lead, shamefacedly went to confront the publican. In tears I apologised profusely for the terrible behaviour of my dog. He laughed and explained that he had only just put the joint in the dustbin as it was time expired. Happy Christmas dog! Sadly I didn't think her digestive system would cope, but I did seriously consider giving it a good wash and serving it up on Boxing Day. It went back in the bin – honestly.

In Stanmore a friend on her way to work picked Kate up miles from home in the middle of the Edgware Road as she caused chaos unconcernedly weaving in and out of the now stationary traffic. The friend thankfully recognised her, opened her car door gave a shout and Kate assumed her usual pose as supreme passenger. The excuse for being late was certainly unique.

When Kate was 11 we were posted to Germany. Our local vet's

heartbreaking advice was to either find a good home for her or have her put down. He reckoned that she would never survive quarantine on our return and as she was fit and healthy might easily live another two or three years. Most of our dog-loving Air Force friends were in the same boat as regards overseas postings. We had civilian friends who lived locally and, although the children and husband were keen to have a dog, the wife had always been adamant that she would never entertain the idea so I didn't even broach the subject.

To my surprise I received a phone call from the lady begging me to let them have the dog, and setting out all the reasons why she felt they could offer her a good home and make responsible pet owners. I was delighted and, of course, agreed. When I questioned the change of heart as regards dog owning the response was simple, 'That's not just any dog, that's Kate!'

BABY ON THE WAY

My waters had broken, our first child was on the way and so we set off to make the 45-mile journey to RAF Hospital Nocton Hall. I did not think I was having contractions and wasn't in much discomfort. We stopped at the traffic lights in Sleaford where, much to my surprise, my husband leapt out of the car saying he was just going to the bank in case he needed cash.

The lights changed, the traffic started hooting, I became embarrassed. So I waddled around the car and into the driver's seat, and then drove round the corner; it was impossible to stop on the double yellow lines in the High Street. Husband duly came out of the bank and quickly realised the car was not there. No one in their right mind would have expected it to be – but this was a special day. I waited for a few minutes and then went to find him. What a sight, he was rushing up and down the High Street in a complete panic shouting that he had lost his wife and that she was having a baby.

Once reunited we continued on our journey, arrived safely and our beautiful daughter was born about an hour later. Just as well we didn't stop much longer!

UNDER THE WEATHER

My husband-to-be was flying the big white triangles from a well-known Lincolnshire base in the early 1960s. He and his crew had departed, together with half of the squadron. They had taken off into a grey, rainy, rotten Lincolnshire afternoon for a four-hour sortie to keep Bomber Command happy.

I had been invited to supper by the wife of my paramour's navigator, with the rest of his crew's ladies. We were thoroughly enjoying our evening, awaiting the return of our menfolk, when the telephone rang. A very apologetic duty officer from the Station Ops desk announced that we were not to expect them home that night. All the aircraft had been diverted due to the weather. A general gloom descended on our little party.

I think we all had another glass or two to drink the health and safe return of our poor suffering airmen. We had no idea where they had been diverted to – and didn't know when they would be coming home. Suddenly, the door opened and my fiancé and his crew appeared! There was much initial joy and hilarity but eventually we demanded an explanation.

'Simple,' said one of the rear crew, looking at me. 'All the rest of the squadron has diverted but, in spite of the weather, your brilliant fella got us home!'

The result – I never again quite believed what Station Ops told me; neither could I support the rumour that my fiancé could possibly have flown under the weather limits.

IN THE BOOT

Routine runway maintenance kept our men on the ground at times and, on one particular occasion, they took refuge in the bar. I can only imagine that one thing led to another, because I heard later that they had taken a door down to use as a base for some drinking game or other.

Some hours later, my doorbell rang. On opening it, I found most of the squadron pouring out of two cars – how on earth they managed it, I'll never know. The guys announced that I was their chosen one – to make bacon butties. All that drinking makes them hungry. They all crowded in and, amidst the chaos in the kitchen, suddenly realised that somebody was missing. Yes, they had left the poor supply officer shut in the boot of one of the cars!

THE WINGS

We had had a fun time in the Royal Air Force. Wife had been happily married to pilot for over twenty years. But one incident led to an interesting revelation. There was a burglary in the household in 1994 and all stolen items needed to be listed ... original cost, date and place of purchase.

As the wife was drawing up the list and filling out the necessary forms to send to the insurers, the details of the stolen 'Wings Brooch' were being filled in. This had been given to her as a birthday present in November 1972, shortly after their marriage.

Wife to husband: 'Darling, do you remember what my Wings Brooch cost?'

Husband: 'I think it was £60 in 1962.'

Wife: 'No, you bought it for me in 1972, for my birthday, just after we married.'

Husband: 'Ah, no, actually I bought the brooch for a former fiancée 10 years earlier. Never let a good thing go to waste!'

Wife, after a few pensive moments: 'Well, at least with the insurance money I can buy my own set of wings and not have to wear second-hand.'

CALM BEFORE THE STORM

We always found family holidays such fun, especially when living in Germany with easy access to the whole of Europe including the Mediterranean coast. We were returning by car from two glorious weeks camping and relaxing away from it all on the Italian coast, but decided to break our journey home in order to visit the picturesque castle of Neuschwanstein (the Chitty Chitty Bang Bang Castle) in Bavaria. The children were excited and raced ahead up the winding track through the woods towards our goal. Suddenly, there were whoops of joy; our son had unexpectedly met his best friend from the base and they were busy swapping holiday tales. Families got chatting and then came the bombshell. 'I thought you would be going to war with your squadron?' said the boy's father.

Out came the whole story that, while we had been away and out of touch with the real world, serious trouble had broken out in the Gulf. There had already been an invasion and there were threats of further attacks. My husband's squadron was being sent out as a task force to help prevent the invasion of other Gulf States. They were due to leave in 48 hours but, since my husband was on leave, they had decided to take another Engineering Officer. Any other details were of little importance. The fact that his men could go to a potential war without him was unthinkable and so that was the end of normal life as we knew it for the next few months.

We did make it up to the castle but he was there only in body, his mind racing as to how quickly he could get home. This was 1990, pre mass mobile phones, so all his communication was effected through the campsite shop; the proprietor was none too enamoured of this intense young man wanting to be constantly on their line in the middle of their busy season. It proved impossible to make contact with his squadron; no one was available until early evening. I persuaded him that a walk with his family around the idyllic lake was probably a good, calming thing to do. Secretly I dreaded that there might never be an opportunity to do it again. The photograph of the children in brilliant sunshine beside the calm, blue lake, with the mountains behind is beautiful, but I can still feel the chill of fear when I look at it.

At about 7.00 that evening contact was made with the squadron. Time was running out so we packed up the remainder of our camping gear and drove solidly for twelve hours through the night. The journey was wretched, both of us tired and emotional, fighting to stay awake, finding it hard to express our feelings and still not sure of what was really happening. Mercifully, the children slept. We arrived at the base around breakfast time. He said he would go to the squadron to find out what was going on, and be back in about an hour; meanwhile I unloaded the car, sorted the children and waited for news. I had to be patient; I waited and waited, anxiety mounting, but trying hard to keep calm and maintaining pretence of normality.

Finally, around tea time, he reappeared with news and no news. He had persuaded the boss that he should go with his men; they were leaving tomorrow, no one knew exactly where they were going, for how long or what to expect, but it was a very serious situation and potentially very dangerous. With rising dread I witnessed his packing of the long green kit bag: two pairs of socks, underwear, gas mask, helmet and Bible; it was a very sobering experience – and with it came the sudden realisation that this wasn't an exercise but was for real. He was at home for an hour. We said our goodbyes after supper and then he was gone.

Two weeks later both children went back to school in England – I was alone.

LONG-DISTANCE OYSTERS

My husband had taken his VC10 to the west coast of America and Canada to support a Nimrod trial. They ended up at RCAF Comox on Vancouver Island in British Columbia. On any overseas deployment the crew always endeavoured to acquire some of the local goodies. The word had been passed around that, for the best

LIVING IN THE SLIPSTREAM

seafood, one should certainly visit 'Portuguese Joe's'. Somewhat dubiously, my husband looked up the said name in the phone directory ... eureka!

He duly visited the establishment armed with several chilled containers and bought some Alaska king crab. He had some Canadian dollars to spare so asked what else was worth buying. The answer – Pacific oysters!

Slightly worried by the idea of bringing fresh oysters home to the UK, he asked, 'Will they last?'

'No problem. Put them in the hotel fridge and then the aircraft fridge and they will be fine.'

They flew back to the UK and he got home at about 2 am. Quite why I was awake I do not know, but I came down in my nightie to welcome him. We sat for the next hour eating the most enormous Pacific oysters, too big to swallow in one go, you had to cut them in half, but they tasted even better than the Sydney rock oysters on which I had been brought up in Oz! We could not manage to eat them all, so rather than waste them; we shared them with our gourmet Labrador.

Dog and humans ended up with smiles on their faces and no ill effects!

THE COLOUR OF MY EYES

Another move and, for my husband, another round of having to collect signatures on the blue arrival card at his new Station. Since I would need a new 'Wife of ...' identity card, the security section needed all my details. My husband managed to supply most of the requirements, including my hair colour and height – however, it was somewhat of a disappointment that he had to phone and ask me the colour of my eyes!

A SURPRISE BIRTHDAY PARTY

Surprise birthday parties can always be risky, but when the very friends who are meant to help keep it a secret are actually the ones who make matters worse, you are on a losing wicket!

My husband's birthday falls around Burns Night in January, and anyone who has served at RAF Leuchars in Scotland will know how seriously Burns Night is taken, with copious amounts of whisky being consumed throughout the night, and the usual hangovers the next day. In this particular year I planned a surprise birthday party for my husband on the Saturday after the Mess's Burns celebrations the night before. A fellow pilot was detailed to collect him that morning, and to keep him out of sight for the rest of the day while I prepared for the party. His instructions were to take him out for a day's golf, and to return him in time for a hot bath before friends arrived to party that evening.

Said friend plus two other chums duly arrived at 10am and collected the birthday boy. They were going to play the Old Course at St. Andrews just down the road, and I am reliably informed that as they arrived in the car park it began to rain. They waited patiently for the rain to ease but, with no let-up in sight, they did what seems to come so naturally to four chaps with time on their hands – they went to the pub.

They arrived back on my doorstep at 4.30, grinning inanely and declaring that they were just coming in for a quick one. Swiftly disabused of that idea by my furious self, they departed with my threats ringing in their ears and my husband dispatched to bed to sober up.

Our friends began to arrive at 8.00 as requested. They knew it was a surprise party, and my notice on the door reminded them to keep quiet. Everyone tiptoed in and spoke in low whispers. Once they were all assembled, I gave the go-ahead for a Raiding Party to go upstairs and surprise my beloved. There was much hooting and roaring, lots of shouting and singing Happy Birthday, and we burst into the bedroom to surprise Birthday Boy.

My husband was still fast asleep in bed, and none of the afore-mentioned noise could wake him. We tried everything, including two of the ladies actually getting into bed with him, but even that seductive ploy failed to attract his attention. I swear the Charge of the Light Brigade could have gone through our house and he would still not have woken up.

And so we gave up and went downstairs to party without him. He therefore missed most of his surprise birthday party, although he did appear some considerable time later that evening to perform his party trick with a pea – but that's another story.

WOULD YOU MIND?

During a particularly busy time for my husband he invited me out into the garden so that he could instruct me in the workings of the lawnmower. This would then allow me, the housekeeper, child minder, chauffeur, domestic goddess, multi-tasker, etc. etc., to relieve him of the job of cutting the grass throughout the coming months.

Happy to learn a new skill (just how difficult is it to mow the lawn?) I listened attentively and absorbed the fascinating facts and technical information.

When he was finished, I politely invited him to join me in the kitchen where I would happily take him through how the cooker, washing machine, tumble drier, dishwasher, microwave, etc. worked. He was not amused!

VALENTINE'S DAY. PART 1: THINK BEFORE YOU BUY

Coming home from work on 14 February, after a hard day defending his country, my dearly beloved dived into the corner shop having totally forgotten the obligatory flowers. Spotting a bucket full of beautiful blooms he asked for a bunch, only to be asked gently if he realised that they were plastic. No he didn't of course but, neither wishing to show his ignorance nor to be defeated, and in mind of 'it's the thought that counts', he bought a bunch and proudly carried it home, presenting it as a loving offering to me.

Well ladies ... in this case, it was NOT the thought that counted. The gift was dreadful! But ...

VALENTINE'S DAY. PART 2: REVENGE IS A DISH BEST SERVED COLD

Several years later, and 300 miles further south, 14 February came round again (as it does).

This time it was my turn. I bought myself a red rose (a real one this time) and, when my husband came home for lunch, thanked him profusely for his kind gesture. I could see he was a little confused, but he covered it well and said that I deserved it ... oh gullible one!

You didn't think I'd leave it there, did you? That evening we were off to the Mess and had invited a few good friends for a drink beforehand. I let my close friend into the secret and primed her as to her role in the forthcoming dénouement.

Glass in hand, she approached my other half and congratulated him for being such a romantic. The poor chap fell right into the trap so carefully laid, repeating that he felt I really deserved it and what else should he do on such a day.

It took some minutes for us to recover from our hysterical laughter and tell him the truth. He then confessed to having been very worried as to where the flower had come from.

WHERE'S THE ROCK?

I had been to Gibraltar many times over the years as my sister owned an apartment on the Costa del Sol in nearby Spain; we had usually taken a cheap charter flight to get there. My husband had flown in and out umpteen times, first in a Vulcan in the 1970s and then in a Nimrod in the 1980s. It was simply another 'day at the office' when he would come home and tell me that he had just returned home via Gibraltar from somewhere more distant.

One day, he surprised me by asking, 'Would you like to go to Gib for the weekend?' He then went on to explain that a C130 was flying there with empty seats and we could take advantage of a late autumn break.

I had never flown in a C130 before, so I saw it as a bit of an adventure – and off we went. It was not the most comfortable flight and even my husband was fidgety.

'I'll just go up to the cockpit and see how they are getting on.' He eased his sore back out of the parachute seat. He obviously felt it would be more comfortable with the crew. On return he said, 'The captain has invited you onto the flight deck for the landing – you'll like that. You will be able to sit on the jump seat.'

I was off in a flash. As I entered the flightdeck there were bright smiles from the crew, but otherwise, nothing to see outside. We were in cloud.

'Just strap in – we'll soon be there. We are just starting the approach – you'll see the Rock in a moment.'

What? But we are in cloud. How could you see anything? How did they know where to look? By now, the temperature had risen. Condensation was dripping from the overhead consoles and indeed the aircrew themselves were dripping a bit, I noticed. I was nervous and there was still no sign of the Rock. And we seemed to be rocking and rolling – a bit too much for comfort, I thought.

'There is often a strong wind here.' The pilot had noticed I was holding on for dear life. 'It can make landing extremely difficult.'

The co-pilot lit a cigarette. Now I knew he was nervous too. Was he going to land the thing? It was all very quiet except for some exchange between the pilot and Air Traffic Control. At least they know where we are I thought.

Just when I was considering saying a prayer, there it was – the

Rock – suddenly on the right hand side. Thank the Lord – we'd missed it.

'There's the runway!' someone called. I peered out. I could make it out very easily and I could also see the end of it – and the sea beyond. Good grief, was the runway long enough? It didn't look at all long enough to me.

We seemed to dive straight for the end … and I closed my eyes. I didn't open them until I felt the familiar bump, bump of a nice smooth landing. I was pretending not to tremble, but actually I was shaking like a jelly. I thanked the good Lord when we were safely down. I had no idea that my nearest and dearest had risked his life so many times!

PASHA AND THE BISHOP

In the 1980s we were stationed at RAF Leuchars where my husband was Station Commander. From time to time we were asked to put up official guests overnight and this anecdote relates to one such occasion.

We were the proud owners of a beautiful black Labrador called Pasha who had been born at RAF Bentley Priory and trained by the mess manager there. Pasha might have had his faults but always warmly greeted guests to the house. On this occasion, however, the arrival of the Roman Catholic Bishop to the Forces and his assistant led to an incident that could never be forgotten.

All went well until, in the midst of a formal dinner, I heard distinct noises emanating from the main guest bedroom above. It transpired that our housekeeper had gone upstairs during dinner to ensure all was well in the bedrooms. To her horror there in the middle of the Bishop's room was a large and very smelly doggy offering.

Copious cleaning could not remove all the remains at the time, so a sheepskin rug was purloined from our son's room to cover the area, and the room sprayed vigorously with air freshener. Our guest never mentioned the matter but must have wondered why his room was suddenly graced with a rug, and filled with the aroma of fake lavender.

Pasha had one further episode with one other visiting senior RAF engineer, but I was quick off the mark on this occasion and averted a repeat performance by changing our guest's sleeping arrangements even as he was mounting the stairs with his luggage. What caused Pasha to take such action on only these two occasions, we shall never know. One may only surmise.

'THE POACHERS' AEROBATIC TEAM

In the early 1970s my husband, while serving at Cranwell as a flying instructor, became a member of 'The Poachers' aerobatic team. Their four aircraft travelled around the UK and Europe and, during the summer months, I was left to hold the reins at home.

Just occasionally, the team performed within a reasonable driving distance and I would bundle the children into the car to support them. However, I soon realised that the image of the team was sometimes dented by the arrival of a harassed mother and a wayward brood.

This was amply demonstrated at one venue when I arrived unexpectedly early, only to find the recently crowned Miss World – Eva Ruber-Staier – sitting on my husband's lap on the wing of his aeroplane! Miss World quickly jumped off the wing and was shepherded away, leaving my husband to explain to me what was going on.

PUNCH IN THE THROAT

I believe we moved nineteen times during our life in the RAF. This was number twelve. My husband, as usual, was away. Quite how he managed to organise a course/detachment for every time we moved I have no idea, but he did. Whether it was by careful planning or sheer luck I will never know. The removal men had picked up the boxes I had packed, loaded all the furniture, and I had completed my 'pre-March Out' house cleaning, exiting the front door backwards on my hands and knees. I finished loading an already full car with a large dog and a very angry cat.

A couple of hours later we arrived at the new quarter along with the removal van and an even angrier cat, to be met by the Families Officer. He was a tall, thin man who struck me as a cross between a mortician and a taxidermist, looking unlikely to have any sense of humour at all. I saw immediately that the house was still full of furniture, but when I mentioned that my husband had requested an empty quarter he sniffed, looked at his clipboard and said I must be wrong. I pointed out that I had a removal van full of furniture, but he sniffed again, referred to the clipboard again and said there was nothing he could do. He then added that this sort of thing always happened when a wife was present at a 'March In'.

As we completed all the paperwork he implied on more than one occasion that I wouldn't understand the details and should just sign – 'Have you ever seen an electricity meter?' I assured him that I had. At this point one of the removal men who had been listening to the conversation took me aside and said that he didn't like the Families Officer and he didn't like the way he was speaking to me. He then asked if I would like him to 'punch him in the throat'. I thanked him for his offer and concern, but suggested it might not help the situation at present. Trying to keep calm, I asked the Families Officer if we could put all the furniture from the house into the garage for the time being, as we really needed to unload the van. He said he supposed we could, but that we had better be careful since, if there was any damage at all, 'You will be charged'! He then left. The removal guys were marvellous, helping to do a double move really, and when all our things were safely in the house they went on their way.

At the end of the weekend, my husband arrived home to a somewhat calmer house with a now contented dog and cat. The furniture had been returned to the store, boxes were all unpacked and removed, pictures up and plants in place. As the new quarter was identical to the one we had just vacated, everything went back into the same place, therefore making the house look just the same as previously.

Before I had a chance to tell him about my week, my husband poured a beer and said happily, 'Well that looks like it was an easy move!' I think at that point I could have cheerfully strangled him, or possibly called that nice removal man back to take up his chivalrous offer.

CARRY ON CAMPING

We were a very friendly squadron stationed at Gutersloh in Germany and often planned activities together at weekends. One particular Friday night after Beer Call a cunning plan was hatched. We had learnt that there was a campsite right in the middle of Amsterdam situated on a football pitch. It was well placed for all the tourist attractions including the red light district of Canal Strasse, which our bachelors would find particularly interesting.

So the following day off we went to camp in Amsterdam. The married couples arrived in good order and, under the usual organisational guidance of the wives, the camp was soon set up. A bottle of wine or two was opened and a few beers drunk as we enjoyed the evening sunshine. Eventually the bachelors turned up and a few more beers were consumed before they decided to put up their tents. The married couples sat back and watched this event unfold.

It soon became obvious that their tents had been borrowed and they didn't have a clue how to erect them. There were poles, pegs, guy ropes, groundsheets and canvas everywhere, and I'm sure they managed to put at least one of them up inside out. The situation was not helped by the ongoing consumption of beer and the not so helpful instructions and laughter from the complacent onlookers.

It only goes to show that every man needs a woman to help him with his tent erection.

'He thinks that's his worst erection!'

AERIAL DESIGNS

Time has moved on since 1966, and physical challenges and mental exercises are all part of the mantra of the Third Age. Mindful of this, I joined a Scottish country dancing group and found myself contemplating the patterns we were making on the floor one session as we 'poussetted', 'figure-of-eighted', and swung our way through a dance. Suddenly I was transported from patterns in a single plane to the three-dimensional ones of the Red Arrows, and back to their first year with nine aircraft.

As they experimented with new ideas for different formations I would occasionally stand at the datum point, the point upon which the whole display is focused, and feed the crowd's 'wow' factor back to the pilots. Sometimes simple comments, such as not putting on the smoke too early, and thus obscuring the next manoeuvre, or making sure that there was always something easily visible for the crowd to enjoy, were considered useful; no aerial expertise was needed here, just an outspoken observer with time to spare. The formations, some with evocative names such as 'Join-up Loop', 'Leader's Benefit', 'Feathered Arrow', 'Roulette', the 'Twinkle' and 'Wineglass' rolls, would be cleverly interwoven and practised to achieve the visually appealing, the unexpected, the terrifying (to the spectators) and the almost unbelievable feats for which the team would become so well known.

When it came to performances of the carefully considered display, Farnborough was the aviation highlight of the year and I eagerly attended, accompanied by family and friends. With a husband in the team, and a few of the wives wearing my custom-made Red Arrow headscarves, I found myself glowing with pride as I watched the show. After the final, thrilling bomb-burst in they came to land and, with horror, I noticed that the first Gnat didn't have its wheels down.

Just in time they appeared and there was a sigh of relief all round. By the time the last aircraft had touched down an announcement was coming over the loudspeakers pointing out that 'Red 1', the team leader, wished it to be known that he always landed last. Guess whose husband had been Red 9 – and guess whose dancing teacher was now reminding her that it was her turn to make a move!

WAR AND THE MOBILE PHONE

Each year our fighter squadrons would go to sunnier climes to practise firing their aircraft's guns. For many years this took place in Malta, then Cyprus, where the skies were a constant blue with barely a cloud to disrupt the training. A Canberra aircraft would tow a large flag behind it and the fighter planes then practise their firing at 'the banner'.

152

This particular year my husband's squadron was to be in Cyprus for most of the school summer holidays, and so we decided that I would take our two teenage children to join him there at the end of the squadron detachment for a family summer holiday. We were very excited and as the day approached our bags were packed, the tickets bought and we were ready to go. However, in August 1990 the news from Iraq was not good and there was definitely trouble brewing. I began to wonder if this would affect our holiday. I tried to convince myself that Cyprus was a long way from Kuwait, that my husband was most unlikely to be involved, and that there was little we would be able to do about Saddam Hussein anyway.

How wrong I was. On the day we were due to depart, the BBC news announced that Saddam Hussein had invaded Kuwait, and that Britain and America were preparing to remove him. Shortly afterwards I got a telephone call from my husband in Cyprus who said that the jets were being fully armed and the squadron was being sent to 'somewhere near Kuwait'. He was not sure where he was going, and I suspect that even if he had known he could not have told me. He did however tell me to cancel the holiday and think of something else to do with the children. During our brief conversation I realised just how serious the situation was. As Squadron Commander he would be leading his squadron into a combat zone where they ran the risk of being shot down. He said he had written me a letter explaining everything, and we then said out tearful goodbyes.

The children were duly told, all the squadron wives were informed, and the holiday flights were cancelled. The following day, after a very sleepless night, I was woken by the doorbell ringing and found the press on my doorstep with cameras at the ready. They wanted to know how I felt, had I spoken to my husband, did I know where they were being sent, and so on. I quickly shut the door. Fortunately the military police managed to get rid of the press, and after a few days the Station set up a wonderful information and support centre for wives and families.

This was a very harrowing time. My husband had actually gone to the huge Saudi Arabian base at Dhahran, just 100 miles or so south of the Iraq/Kuwait border, and the squadron flew patrols along the Iraqi border around the clock. One day I saw him being interviewed on the BBC and, to my horror, he was wearing a gun in a holster over his shoulder. I remembered him telling me years before, during the Cold War against the Soviet Union, that guns were only issued to aircrew so that, in the event of being shot down and safely ejecting, they could shoot themselves rather than be captured by the enemy. I always suspected that this was said tongue in cheek, at least I hoped so, but I was never sure and I certainly did not see it as a joke at this particular time.

I also received his farewell letter at about the same time which again reduced me to tears. However, I kept busy looking after the other wives as we all tried to comfort each other and make the best of the situation.

We take them for granted today, but in 1990 mobile phones were in their infancy and were just beginning to be sold to the general public. Because land lines and military phone lines could be tapped, everyone was reminded of the dangers of loose talk on the phone and that we should all be very careful what was said in case sensitive information got into the wrong hands. Those of us back at Base therefore resigned ourselves to the fact that there would be no contact with our husbands, and that we would be dependent on the BBC news to tell us what was going on, just like everyone else. We were glued to every bulletin.

Imagine my delight when I got a phone call one evening from my husband, who told me that they had been accommodated in the British Aerospace compound in Dhahran. The BAe personnel had been evacuated back to the UK, so the aircrew were able to move in to their accommodation, lock, stock and mobile phone. The mobile phone my husband used was apparently the size of a brick, but it kept us in daily contact at the most stressful time of our lives. I was able to pass on messages to the other wives, and sometimes to speed up information to the official support team on Base. I remain ever grateful that that particular piece of technology came into being when it did.

LOST

While living in Ramstein, Germany, and at the end of my time teaching English as a foreign language to Eastern Bloc air traffic controllers in Budapest, one of my students invited me to stay in his idyllic cottage high in the Tatras mountains near Ostrava in Slovakia. He made it sound very romantic, showing me photos of his little wooden chalet and explaining that it was miles from anywhere. In fact, there were no made up roads within miles and the only way to it was on foot. He went on to explain that his favourite pastime there was collecting wild mushrooms. It all sounded like a fairy tale and I was really keen to go and see this Hansel and Gretel cottage.

At about the same time a navigator friend, who had a private pilot's licence and access to a four-seater light aircraft, was encouraging my husband, who was a pilot, to join him as his navigator on a flight to Prague and beyond. It was agreed that we would fly to Prague, stay overnight and then fly on to Ostrava.

It all seemed a very good idea at the time. After a great deal of planning the navigator and his wife, together with my husband and me, set forth in what seemed to me to be a very small aircraft. Our overnight stay in Prague went without incident and we made it safely to Ostrava. There my student, who had arranged to be the duty air traffic controller that day, met us and took us by car to the edge of the woods, pointing out the track that led to his cottage.

An hour's walk later we emerged into a clearing, halfway up a mountain, to find a little hamlet and the tiny wooden chalet. It was perched on the hillside overlooking a beautiful valley, complete with a stable door, gingham curtains and wooden shutters with heart shapes cut out; it fitted one's image of a Hansel and Gretel scene absolutely perfectly.

155

The following day was just as perfect and, with the sun shining, we set forth on a thirty-minute descent into the valley in search of the mushrooms he had told me about. After eating our picnic and gathering our mushrooms, we decided to take a different route back.

We did have a map but the new path we had chosen seemed to be quite visible, so no problem. It was at this point that the weather seemed to change and clouds started to roll in as we trudged back up the hill. After an hour's walking the sun went in and we began to feel quite chilly having not brought any extra clothing to cover our shorts and T-shirts. After two hours, we entered a seriously dense wooded area and began to realise that we had probably taken the wrong path. After three hours, we girls began to make thinly disguised, disparaging remarks about the navigational skills of two of Her Majesty's Finest. It was now beginning to get very cold and the men joked that if the worst came to the worst we could always stay the night in the woods by making a shelter and lighting a fire. Not a great prospect in view of the wild bears that reputedly roamed those particular woods, so we continued to walk in what we thought to be the right direction, following our heroes.

After four hours struggling through this thick forest, the men huddled over the map and I overheard one say, 'If only we could see the sun we could establish north and orientate the map properly.'

I paused, chose my moment and said, 'Moss always grows on the north side of trees, so what's the problem?' The fully trained pilot and vastly experienced navigator, who had both spent many a night on various survival training exercises with the RAF, looked at me incredulously.

The map was duly orientated, we worked out where we were, made it straight back onto our path, instantly recognised familiar territory and made it back to the cottage without further ado.

Thank goodness for the Brownies.

ZORBIN

I have always thought that the RAF motto should have been 'Haven't you heard, it's all been changed' – known colloquially as 'Zorbin', as in 'zorbin changed'. I lost count many years ago of how many times I was let down by my husband's last minute change of plans thanks to the RAF.

After weeks away on detachment, sometimes in good places sunning themselves on a beach, or sometimes in not such good places like war zones, the long awaited and much anticipated return would be imminent, and some very excited wives would make every effort to welcome back their conquering heroes in fine style. Like the time we dressed up as Bunny Girls on a freezing cold winter's day, with champagne at the ready as they walked back into the squadron. Such welcoming parties were common and became more elaborate the longer the detachment. On one occasion it had been a particularly long nine-month detachment while the runway was being resurfaced, and we were given a false alarm for their return on three separate occasions, but decided to continue to celebrate on our own anyway. One soon learnt not to count on their return until they actually walked through the door, but try explaining that to some very excited kids!

Following the reception at the squadron it then became customary to push the boat out in order to impress one's husband on arrival at home by having prepared a sumptuous meal. Money was extremely tight in the 1970s but the very best steak was one way of creating the right impression, even if we could ill afford it. This was when the Zorbin effect came into play, because first we were informed that our husband would be back that morning, then that afternoon, then it became that evening, which rapidly became tomorrow. The following day as often as not it was a similar story. This turn of events could sometimes go on for days and even weeks. Often an aircraft would break down en route and get stuck at some foreign backwater, or the weather was too bad, or certain foreign air traffic control would not allow them into their airspace, and so on.

Meanwhile, at home the steak was defrosted and had to be put back in the fridge. The following day it would be resurrected and we would try again, a procedure that might continue until the steak was unfit for human consumption. Finally husband would return, a new steak would be served in all its splendour, only to be met with the words 'oh steak again' as he explained that he had been eating steak for the past week. Happy days!

8

Pomp and Circumstance

A ROYAL VISIT

It was in the mid-1980s, while my husband was Station Commander at a fighter base in eastern England, that we had a formal visit from a Royal Personage. On the morning of the luncheon I invited the wing commanders' wives to join me at home for a relaxing sherry. We were just taking our first sip when I received a frantic phone call to say the whole programme was progressing faster than expected, so we were to be driven to the Mess NOW. Quick pennies were spent and off we sped.

On arrival we stood in our allocated groups and were duly introduced to our royal guest; then on into the dining room. When a Royal visits, the chairs at the top table have to be placed much further apart than normal – which was a blessing in disguise as it turned out! Our royal guest sat between my husband and me, with the equerry on my left. The menus had been sent to the royal household and noisettes of lamb with Parisienne potatoes were selected for the main course.

HRH chatted to me for part of the first course and while the main course was being served. This was my undoing, as I was not paying attention to how many potatoes were being put on my plate by the steward. Our guest then turned to my husband to talk about aircraft while I was able to chat to the equerry. I started cutting my lamb and my knife slipped. Whoops! My potato balls hit the side of the equerry's chair (luckily a very deep G-Plan seat), and shot under the table and across the royal blue carpet behind me, just where our guest would walk when leaving.

The equerry by this time was shaking with laughter. 'Don't you dare tell him,' I said. His eyes twinkled in reply. I had a quick glance to my right but our guest was still chatting to my husband. Phew! Then I anxiously looked down the dining room but nobody appeared to have seen the incident. I sat there for what seemed like an age when I felt something at my feet – it was a steward on his hands and knees with his silver salver, picking up my potato balls! He then stood behind me with the salver raised to shoulder level. I prayed that I wouldn't be served my retrieved Parisienne potatoes. I still had the worry of HRH treading the potatoes behind me all through the Mess, but all was well – they too had been picked up.

You can guess what kind of potatoes we were served at my husband's dining out night!

A RIGHT ROYAL MIX-UP

In November 1990 our camp in RAFG emptied of almost all its serving personnel as Operation Desert Storm began. The wives left behind were looked after extremely well by the remaining staff and the local community. Various outings and treats were arranged, and each morning the CO held a briefing in the Malcolm Club to keep us informed of the latest news from the war zone, before it was broadcast more widely.

One morning, we heard that Jasper Carrot and Nigel Kennedy were giving a concert at an army base about three hours' drive from us. It was to be held that evening and sixty tickets had been sent to our station for anyone wishing to attend. Names were taken there and then. After most of the tickets had been spoken for there were a few left for the officers' wives, so my friend and I decided it would be a concert well worth six hours in a military bus.

Later that afternoon two buses filled up with excited women, all looking forward to the outing. My friend and I had decided that such a long drive required comfortable clothing, and we were not alone in choosing jeans and jumpers as suitable for the trip. The bus 'monitor' was a young flight lieutenant who seemed a little daunted at the task of escorting such a large group of females.

All went well until about two hours into the journey, when we noticed that we had lost the second bus. After doubling back, we saw it on the hard shoulder of the autobahn, having broken down. The poor bus monitor was flummoxed, until we decided to cram everyone onto our bus (Health and Safety look away now!). We arrived at the army camp, late, with half of the passengers sitting on our laps!

Just as we were about to creep into the concert, which was now well under way, the long-suffering monitor remembered he hadn't given us our tickets. He rushed up and down the bus handing out tickets of three different colours without any thought or explanation. My friend and I, and all sitting near us, had blue ones, but others had red or green. We entered the hall just before Nigel Kennedy began to play his famous rendition of Vivaldi's 'Four Seasons', and we all thoroughly enjoyed the performance.

When it had finished, an announcement was made. 'Will all people with green tickets please go to the NAAFI for tea and sandwiches, all people with red tickets please go to the Sergeants' Mess for refreshments, and all blue ticket holders please visit the Officers' Mess anteroom.'

We realised our tickets had been mixed up, but no one seemed to mind, and we led a group of SAC's wives into the Officers' Mess for champagne and canapés, while the other officers' wives headed to the NAAFI for their supper. It was only when we arrived in the Mess, in our jeans and trainers, mixing with the army wives in their twinsets and pearls, and were shepherded into a receiving circle, that we realised that Prince Edward had attended the concert, and was moving round the room visiting each group. He wasn't at all fazed to greet our raggle-taggle group, and seemed amused to hear our story, I'm sure we appreciated his visit more than most and it made a fine tale to tell later!

The bus monitor was strangely quiet on the way home.

A ROYAL PROMPT

As mothers we have all experienced the agony of our young when expecting them to be on their 'best behaviour'. They do need a little coaching and priming from time to time.

One of my most memorable moments was being invited to a reception hosted by Princess Diana at Kensington Palace. She was accompanied by Prince William, who must have been 10 or 11 years old at the time and who would be making his first public speech. I imagine that Diana was as nervous as her son, for she did what so many mothers do to help their offspring on such occasions – she mouthed every word with him.

THE DUKE AND THE CHRISTMAS TREE

The build-up to Christmas had been more hectic than normal and we had been out seventeen nights in a row, culminating in the Christmas party in the mess. It was a very good evening and as usual we were almost the last to leave. As we got into bed my husband set the alarm and said he had to get up early next day to say farewell to the Duke of York whose aircraft had landed on the air base that evening in order to collect him from a function he was attending in York. It is customary for a station commander to welcome visiting royalty to his Station and also to bid farewell at the end of a visit by standing smartly to attention at the appointed hour and saluting as the royal guest boards the aircraft.

My husband was up early that morning and disappeared off to do the farewell bidding, while I remained in bed recovering from the night before. He took up his duty position on the tarmac ready to give his farewell salute. However, on this occasion the Duke's aircraft failed to start. A few moments later, the Duke popped his head out of the aircraft and said, 'Station Commander, it's going to take a while to fix this problem, can we go to your residence for coffee?'

Meanwhile I am lying in bed and finding it very difficult to raise my head from the pillow. I remember that we have a very large Christmas tree lying in our entrance hall and I really ought to get up to sort that out, and anyway I need to go out to do some grocery shopping. Suddenly I get a phone call from my husband who says, 'I'm bringing him home for coffee.'

'Who?'

'The Duke of course.'

It's strange what goes through your head at times like that. All I could think of was, what shall I wear, we have no biscuits, and should I curtsey. I have never got dressed so quickly in all my life, hair all over the place, no time to wash, and no make-up. I threw on a clean pair of jeans and a pretty top, and thought it better to look

163

casual and create the impression I was used to royalty dropping by every day. I negotiated the Christmas tree in the hall, moved it to one side so that he could at least get through the front door, put the kettle on, hunted for some not-so-stale biscuits and waited.

Just as I had done all that, the doorbell rang. I leapt up in nervous anticipation – only to discover that it was my husband, on his own. The aircraft had been fixed in short order by our usual super-efficient RAF groundcrew, and the Duke was gone. Relieved as I was, I was left wondering whether, dressed as I was, I would have curtseyed or not?

ROYAL LOO PAPER

It was the early 1990s, and my husband had recently taken on his dream job: Station Commander of a busy operational airfield in Germany. He had a big office, a smart car and driver, lots of people hanging on his every word, and (best of all) lots of flying whenever he wanted in a range of different aircraft! This was more than he had ever dreamed of when he joined up, and it's fair to say that he was feeling pretty pleased with himself.

The first Gulf War had recently ended; the troops and the squadrons had returned to their bases, and a Drumhead Service in Remembrance and Thanksgiving was to be held at Munster for the Germany-based units. The Prince and Princess of Wales were attending and large numbers of politicians and the Great and Good were flying out from the UK in a Tristar. Our base was relatively close to Munster; as an air trooping centre, we had a big air movements facility, so we were the obvious choice as an airhead.

The great day dawned, the buses were lined up round the back, the Tristar was reported as being on schedule, and we waited in the 'VIP Lounge' of our air movements centre: room for half a dozen chairs, a table with paper doilies for the biscuits, and access to a posh toilet – which we anticipated might be needed by some of our visitors before their bus trip. Waiting with us (together with a host of anxious Movements Staff, taciturn RAF police, and chatty stewards with coffee pots at the ready) were the Commander in Chief (CinC) and his wife, ready to greet the greatest of the VIPs as they disembarked. Just as the Tristar was on final approach to land, Lady CinC excused herself and disappeared into the toilet – from where she emerged a minute later to whisper to me that the solitary toilet roll on view was just about to run out. My husband takes up the story ...

When my wife told me about our impending toilet paper disaster, I thought, 'No problem. I shall snap my fingers, and a myriad of underlings will be at my beck and call to remedy matters in an instant.' On looking around, however, I saw only a concerned wife, an expectant Lady CinC, and a preoccupied CinC gathering his bits and pieces together in preparation for taking his place by the aircraft steps. The anxious Movements Staff, the taciturn RAF police, even the chatty stewards with coffee pots (where the HELL had they gone?) had all melted away. And the Tristar had just turned off the runway.

A brief 'Excuse me, Sir; I'll be with you in one moment' to the CinC; a quick look around the toilet for any fresh supplies hiding anywhere, a momentary impulse to try passing off the doilies as the very latest fashion in German toilet paperware, and I was out of the lounge and galloping across the hangar towards the gents in the squaddies' departures area. I raided a couple of cubicles (not exactly 'Duvet in the Bathroom' quality, but any port in a storm) and another 100-yard sprint back to the lounge, heart pounding, medals jangling, and clutching two rolls of IZAL Imperial Impervious – to be met by the stewards, back with fresh coffee. 'Refill, Sir?'

'No ... thank you,' through gritted teeth, as I threw my precious cargo at them and rushed out to join everyone else at the steps, just as the Tristar doors opened.

Lessons learned? First: pride comes before a fall. Second: the reassurance that, if I got sacked as a station commander, I could always make it as a toilet attendant. Third: the Great and Good must have iron constitutions – not a single one of them needed the loo!

IMPERIAL CAVIAR

It was during the 1970s that my husband had just returned from flying Princess Margaret to Teheran to visit the Shah of Persia. In those days the crew were allowed to bring home any uneaten victuals from their flights. On this particular occasion he brought home a one-pound tin of Imperial Caviar which he proudly presented to me. When I opened it, I couldn't help but exclaim, 'Some swine has taken a whole teaspoon's worth out of this!'

My husband gently explained that Princess Margaret had been the culprit!

AN AWKWARD CURTSEY

While living at RAF Northolt in the 1980s, I would enjoy trips to London to see the latest exhibitions. One year a friend and I went to see the Summer Exhibition at the Royal Academy. A particular picture caught my attention and, as I focused on it, I took a couple of backward steps. Much to my horror, I reversed straight into Her Majesty the Queen.

Looking on, my friend discreetly retired a few paces away, watching as I converted my embarrassment into an immediate curtsey – an Australian with a very red face.

THE ROYAL MEDALS

In the early 1970s we were posted to RAF Stafford and I became involved with the nursery school. We had approximately forty children in the school, who were a delightful bunch of bright and lively toddlers. As always there are the characters and one such child was a little boy called Alex. Alex was into everything and always wanted to help everyone with whatever they were doing at the time. He always had so many tales to tell of what went on in his life, some of which were very amusing and at times some which should not have been repeated. The thing about Alex was that he wore large white NHS glasses and he also had one ear higher than the other, so his mother wrapped Elastoplast around one arm of the spectacles so that they sat evenly on his face.

The station was due to have a royal visit and a programme was planned to tidy up and make everything look perfect for the VIP. After everything had been organised and put into action and

'Hey missus! You been collecting Shell petrol medals?'

rehearsals had taken place, the Station Commander decided that the whole station looked too clinical and lacked atmosphere. It was decided that the children from the nursery school would line the route and be given little 'union jacks' to wave as the procession passed on its way to the Officers' Mess.

The big day came and Princess Alice Duchess of Gloucester arrived at RAF Stafford. The children lined the side of the road and were told that when the big black car came into view they all had to cheer very loudly and wave their flags. No one expected the car to stop, that was not on the itinerary, but to everyone's surprise Princess Alice requested that she meet the enthusiastic youngsters. The moment she alighted the vehicle, Alex could hardly contain his excitement. Here was a lady in RAF uniform and she was heading straight for him. On her uniform she was wearing various medals and these had caught his eye. As she drew level with him and bent down to talk to him, he flicked the medals on her chest with his flag and asked, 'Hey missus, have you been collecting Shell petrol medals as well?'

The Station Commander looked mortified but the Duchess was still giggling as she got back into the car and continued on her way to lunch.

GIN AND TONIC

The headquarters of No 11 Group was at Bentley Priory in Stanmore. This historic building, from which Dowding and Churchill had directed the Battle of Britain, was gutted by fire in the early 1980s. After its refurbishment Her Majesty the Queen Mother had been invited to re-open the building.

On this grand occasion there was to be a formal lunch, preceded by drinks in the anteroom, where the Queen Mother would have the opportunity to meet as many of her hosts as possible. To that end we were assembled all around the anteroom in groups of about ten. So, with more than 100 people present, the Queen Mother had over ten groups to spend time with if she was to meet everyone – or should I say, if we were all to have the chance to meet her.

Each of our groups had a 'leader' whose job it was to introduce those in his company to Her Majesty. We were all in place in good time, each with a drink in hand, so that when she entered the room introductions could begin without interruption by stewards. Furthermore, our brief had been that as soon as the Queen Mother had left your group, you were all to slip out of the anteroom quietly and take your places in the dining room ready for the lunch.

We were in the last group to be presented. Everything seemed to be going very well and the programme was even running on time. Those already presented had discreetly left the room and the Air Marshal accompanying Her Majesty looked particularly happy as he escorted her towards the final group. Introductions were effected, then, as soon as she had dutifully shaken hands with the last in our group, the Air Marshal announced that lunch was now served and invited her to follow him.

'Oh,' she said. 'It's all right for you, but where's my gin and tonic?'

While we had been sipping our aperitifs steadily throughout the whole time she had been touring the anteroom, no one had thought to offer our Royal guest a drink! A gin and tonic was hastily produced and she spent a few more minutes chatting to us while she drank it. It made our day. What a lovely lady.

OOH, A FLYPAST

In the early 1990s the RAF Benevolent Fund invited Princess Margaret to open Rothbury House, a respite centre in Northumberland for the benefit of RAF families. My husband was Station Commander at RAF Leeming in Yorkshire at the time, and he was tasked to provide a flypast at Rothbury House to mark the occasion. The resident Hawk aircraft of 100 Squadron were selected for the honour, and the Royal Party and VIPs all made their way to Rothbury.

I remember the weather on the day as being absolutely atrocious – strong winds, low cloud and torrential rain. My husband never seemed to be off the phone back to Base as he kept seeking updates on whether the flypast would be able to go ahead or not. That part of Northumberland is particularly hilly, and anything but reasonable weather would have made it too dangerous for the aircraft to fly low enough for a flypast.

We were all introduced to Her Royal Highness, tea was served, and there was a tour of the facilities, which I must admit were most impressive. At the end of the tour we arrived in a very long room at the top of the building with views from one end to the other, an ideal viewing point for the flypast if it were able to take place.

Princess Margaret was very easy to talk to, which was just as well because there were a few minutes to wait before the flypast was due. It became clear that she too considered the weather too bad for low flying and gave the impression that she had put the flypast completely out of her mind. Just then, my husband rushed over from the window at the far end of the room to which he had been glued, on the lookout for the blazing landing lights of four low-flying Hawks. He calmly said by way of an announcement, 'Excuse me Ma'am, but if you would like to come to the far window you will see a flypast of Hawks,' whereupon Her Highness's face lit up. She literally sprinted to the window, excitedly declaring, 'Ooooh a flypast, I love flypasts!'

And so it was. The Hawks had done outstandingly well just to find Rothbury House in those conditions, but in so doing made one member of the Royal Family very happy, and one RAF wife exceedingly relieved. Well done chaps.

9

Paid and Unpaid Work

THRIFT SHOP ANTICS

I always found it great fun working in the Thrift Shop, which frequently provided much amusement. On one occasion a lady brought in a breast pump. One of our gallant sales team then began to describe in graphic detail how she had once become totally stuck in such an appliance. The picture she painted was hilarious and we were falling about with laughter unable to control ourselves. The pump was put on display but we were doubtful that it would be sold.

The inevitable happened; a fresh-faced young man picked it up, carried it over to the desk, money in hand and enquired if it still worked. Trying to keep a straight face, I responded that as far as I knew it was very effective. Unfortunately the same team was on duty and the mere sight of the appliance reduced them to hysterics. The young man was very perplexed and fled the shop clutching his purchase, while I too collapsed in a fit of giggles.

SOUTH ATLANTIC SUMMER BALL

One Monday morning at work I was asked what I had done that weekend, to which I replied that I had been to a summer ball in the South Atlantic. This was looked upon with great scepticism, until I explained that my husband was in the RAF and that Ascension Island was under his command.

We flew down on the Thursday night to arrive early on Friday morning. We attended the ball that evening had a leisurely day on the Saturday, watched turtles burying their eggs in the sand in the evening and flew back to Brize Norton arriving early on Sunday morning. What a long way to go for a party!

THE SCIENCE TEACHER

Understandably as a domestic science teacher who was teaching pure science I was not given the top-grade examination class. Instead I was asked to teach a class of 14–15-year-old less-able pupils who needed extra help. They were a challenging bunch and very streetwise. Most of them had moved house and schools at least six times with their army parents and had probably lived in several countries.

One gloriously hot day near the end of term I decided to take the class to the local park for a nature walk. I asked the pupils to collect as many bugs as they could and put them in the containers I had provided so that we could identify them later. They were given ten minutes for this exercise, during which time I found a bench near a formal pool with a gentle bubbling fountain. As I relaxed it all went very quiet, then the gentle bubbling fountain suddenly shot fifty feet into the air; there was much giggling from behind the bushes. My not-so-smart class had been smart enough to discover the fountain's controls and how they worked.

Walking the class back to school I noticed that one of the boys had a wet trouser pocket. I asked him how he had got wet, thinking it was something to do with the fountain. Rather sheepishly, he put his hand into his pocket and pulled out a rather large and very dead Koi carp.

'Is this what you wanted us to collect, Miss?'

THE BOSS'S WIFE

When a wife follows her husband from place to place in the RAF it is taken very much for granted that she will conform to the requirements of his job in order to support him in whatever he is doing at the time. As his career advances and he is given more responsibility, he tends to rely more and more on his wife's taking on the more mundane aspects of everyday life, often without noticing that it is happening. At one stage I was asked what it was like to be the Boss's wife and, after a short pause, I likened it to being his hand-bag. I was taken out to lunches, dinners and receptions, I was kept on-hand when required, I was most useful when consulted for dates, lists, other wives' names, ailments, birthdays, etc. and was always close by when required.

But once the evening progressed I was quietly put down in a safe corner and left completely unattended, such that, by the end of the evening he would quite forget where he had left me!

ANOTHER GENERATION

During the last decade of the twentieth century a conference was held at RAF Brampton for very senior officers, and I, as the wife of a PSO (Personal Staff Officer, Private Secretary) to one of the delegates, was invited to join the ladies' programme.

Our day was wonderfully organised with a private viewing of a National Trust property and its beautiful gardens, followed by a very nice lunch. On our return to Brampton we were ushered into the Officers' Mess for a debrief on the discussion by the great and the good of the Air Force. It was all very informal over a glass of wine.

One of the senior ladies, who must have been near retirement age, remarked how awful it was that young wives 'these days' seemed to 'want to work'. She felt that wives of officers should not be allowed to work. As I was not quite 40 years of age, I piped up that I considered that my generation was probably the last of the 'stay at home' wives and that modern Air Force wives were often highly qualified and wanted to work and be financially independent.

'I don't think so, dear,' she replied firmly.

BREAST FEEDING

In 1994 I was a newly promoted wing commander and the first nursing mother to attend the RAF Advanced Staff Course. On my first day I was taken aside by the Deputy Commandant. Clearly, he knew nothing of nannies and expressed milk, as he proceeded to gain my assurance that there would be no breast feeding in the auditorium.

MATERNITY WEAR

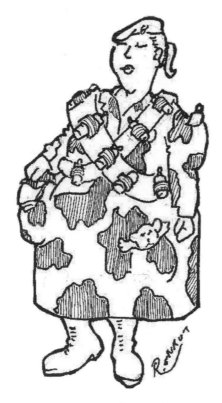

Combat ready

In the early 1990s the military had to adjust to the prospect of pregnant women. At the time, I was Personal Staff Officer for a member of the Air Force Board. Towards the end of this tour I became pregnant. At first we were allowed to wear civilian clothes during pregnancy. However the army, which was responsible for clothing policy, decided that a tri-service pregnancy uniform should be trialled.

In due course I was approached to 'do a twirl' for the Air Force Board in the new uniform designed by our army colleagues. My spirits sank as I donned what appeared to be a bell-tent, festooned with pockets, which was sure to attract derision and mirth in equal measure. My first 'twirl' triggered wry humour from a bemused Board. Someone then asked the purpose of the many pockets. Apparently, the pockets reflected the army view that pregnant women could never have too many pockets for their 'women's things'. At this my boss could contain himself no longer and in a terrible rage fumed that knowing the army they were probably for carrying ammo.

With this the Air Force Board lost its corporate composure and, so far as I know, at that time the RAF lost any interest in uniforms for its pregnant ladies.

WRAF GOES FLYING

In the early 1980s I was stationed at RAF Digby where I shared a married quarter with my husband, who was Engineering Officer on the Lightning Training Flight (LTF). My husband often flew in the two-seat Lightning, as it was frequently used as a single seater and therefore had a spare seat he could occupy.

One day the 'boys' asked me if I should like a trip. Of course I would! The Boss was approached but despite authorising occasional flights for female air traffickers (lumpy jumpers) he decided that a flight by me would amount to flagrant nepotism.

A few weeks later I learned that the Boss would be on leave and that my husband, who had the same surname and rank as me, would be authorised to fly; if I were to be available in his place then no lies need be told. So it was that this WRAF officer flew in the Lightning.

NATURE TAKES THE LEAD

As part of our officer training/selection we had to display our leadership qualities during a series of camps on various rather depressing army ranges. On this occasion we were told that we mere cadets would be sharing the range with Ghurkhas and that we must not interrupt their important work. After several days suffering from the usual compo ration constipation, I realised that salvation would be coming to me during a night-ex. I tried to find solitude and some cover for my activity on this particularly barren bit of Norfolk heath.

After inventing some reason for my urgent desire to leave the men of my flight, I rushed for the cover of the nearest tree. Undressing was not simple as I had to remove nuclear, biological and chemical protective clothing and then DPM trousers, long johns and then my womanly M&S knickers. My 'unloading' took as long to complete and a helpful bit of moonlight played revealingly on the only part of my anatomy not covered in cam cream.

Taking sometime to re-dress, I heaved a sigh of relief – and was shocked to hear my tree do the same and move off away from me, to avoid further despoiling of his army-issue boots. Fortunately, he disappeared into the gloom along with my constipation ...

INSIDER INFORMATION

During the Balkan war my husband was in the thick of the Intelligence world. It was a difficult time and he worked extremely long hours.

It so happened that my 'daily' was from the old Yugoslavia and she and her husband had left their homeland about five or six years earlier to make a new life in England. She was proud of their transition and particularly pleased that their children had settled in well at an English-speaking school. Her husband had a 'good job' and she was probably the best cleaning lady I ever had.

At the time, NATO was bombing selected military targets in the heart of Belgrade and this practice was severely criticised, particularly after a bomb had gone astray causing civilian casualties and damage to civilian property. It was all very sensitive and the press would delight in examining the strategy of the NATO commanders.

I found myself asking my 'daily' what she thought about the bombing; she was never slow in coming forward. I was surprised to learn that she was able to contact her family in Belgrade with ease. Apparently the telephone system still functioned in spite of the turmoil in the city. By now my husband too was interested to hear, first hand, of the reactions of her family to the bombing. She would therefore telephone either her parents or other relatives every evening to ensure that they were still all right and to find out how the attacks were being received. It was always encouraging to hear from our cleaning lady that her friends in Belgrade were confident of the accuracy of NATO's bombing strikes and that they, as civilians, rarely felt threatened.

DISCRIMINATION

'How long will you be here for?'

In the 1970s laws on sex discrimination were not well established. I was a science graduate, desperate to work, and so applied for many jobs. I had many interviews which went something along these lines: 'We see you live at RAF … how long will you be here for? What does your husband do? Are you planning to have children?'

In the early days I was sufficiently naive to proudly say that yes, my husband was an Engineering Officer, we lived in the married quarters, we did not know how long he would be there, and that we were not planning to start a family. Eventually I became more devious – if possible I made no mention of the Royal Air Force in my address and when questioned further was fairly vague about the exact location. My husband became just an engineer and it was always a permanent move. However prospective employers usually managed to work it out and were sufficiently biased to tell me on several occasions that I was well qualified and would fit the position perfectly, if it wasn't for the fact that my husband was in the Air Force.

ALL CHANGE

I am sitting in the garden of our married quarter quietly congratulating myself that all is in order for our forthcoming move in ten days' time, back to our own house in Rutland. It will be the first time we have ever been able to live in our own home and I am very excited. The tenants have moved out of our house, the removals are booked, I have handed in my notice and after several interviews have managed to secure myself another job in my line of work, including a promotion, in a neighbouring town, but most importantly – and again for the first time – it will be just down the road from where our children are in boarding school. Life is looking good.

Husband arrives home. 'Do you want the good news or the not so good?'

The good news is that he is being offered one of the very few posts for engineering officers as a station commander, a very special job with lots of prestige and wonderful social opportunities for us both. Not to mention the nice married quarter, some domestic help and a driver, along with a factory for him to run as well as an RAF Station. The not so good news is that the posting is with immediate effect, and it is on the other side of the country. Sadly we will not be living close to the children and will face another long and difficult journey to see them. I need to find more tenants for our home as soon as possible as we still have to pay the mortgage. Bang goes my new job – I know I'm not going to be very popular with my new employers and have to pluck up courage to tell them I won't be coming.

What is there to say other than 'Yes?'

Once I had recovered from the shock I eagerly anticipated my new role and home. Hey presto, we were off to Wales in a week.

10

Final Reflections

AN AIR FORCE WIFE

An Air Force wife is mostly a girl.

But there are times, such as when her husband is away and she is mowing the lawn or fixing a flat tyre on a youngster's bike, that she begins to suspect she is also a boy.

She usually comes in three sizes: petite, plump and pregnant. During the early years of her marriage it is often hard to determine which size is her normal one.

An ideal Air Force wife has the patience of an angel, the flexibility of putty, the wisdom of a scholar and the stamina of a horse.

She is sentimental, carrying her memories with her in an old vanity case.

She is above all a woman, who married a man, who offered her the permanency of a gypsy, the miseries of loneliness, the frustrations of conformity and the security of love.

Sitting among her packing boxes with squabbling children nearby, she is sometimes willing to chuck it all in, until she hears the firm footstep and cheerful voice of that man who gave her all this.

Then, she is happy to be – his Air Force wife.

A WORLD WAR II SURVIVOR

When an RAF Station closes, as well as the land and the buildings being sold off, all the equipment, including everything in married

quarters, is counted, checked against an inventory and either sold or returned to store. As one might imagine, despite careful accounting, there is great potential for things to go astray. So now it's confession time.

After nearly twenty years, I admit my guilt. Nothing disappeared from within the Station Commander's residence, where I was living at the time – there was nothing I wanted to salvage from that house, certainly not that boring crockery or utilitarian cutlery that had already seen long service. There was nothing on the inventory there that I might allow, unobtrusively, to find its way into our packing cases, despite hints that it would probably all be thrown out anyway.

But there was just one thing that I 'rescued'; in the potting shed there was a watering can. Or rather, in the language of RAF inventories: 'Can, watering, CO's garden for the use of.' It's a sturdy, old-fashioned, metal watering can and, astonishingly, it has a crown embossed on it and bears the marking 'GR 1942'. I've always wondered about that watering can. How did it manage, in 1942, not to be melted down and made into a Spitfire? And I've often wondered about who used it. I imagine some gardener in 1942, digging for victory and tending the patriotic vegetable patch where the rose garden used to be before the war. I imagine someone filling the watering can and using it to water carrots, perhaps, bending down to inspect their progress. And then as a familiar sound is heard overhead, perhaps the gardener would straighten up and gaze at the sky to see Lancasters or Halifaxes overhead, and would mutter a silent prayer for their safe return. It's an odd thing to keep, a watering can, but I treasure it.

CARRY ON REGARDLESS

In the early 1990s, my husband was CO of JARIC (Joint Air Reconnaissance Intelligence Centre) at RAF Brampton. It was the day of the Annual Reception and all the usual arrangements had been made to host our many guests, both military and civil.

It was a warm, sunny day which boded well for the evening cocktail party which was to be held on the lawns to the rear of the Officers' Mess. We had been lucky to secure the Central Band of the Royal Air Force to attend and play for us throughout the evening. Our officers from all three services and numerous civilian staff, had been briefed on their hosting duties and the mess manager, waiters and stewards were fully prepared with all the catering arrangements.

But, a setback! As final preparations were being made during the late afternoon, my husband was informed that the band would not be able to make it. Their coach had been involved in a road traffic accident on the M25 en route to us from their HQ at RAF Uxbridge; they were, understandably, in no fit state to serenade us that night! This was a bit of a blow. The loss of military music to accompany our reception was a great disappointment but, never mind, no one had been seriously injured and that was the main thing.

However, there would be a slight dilemma. Normally, towards the end of a cocktail party such as this, after the RAF Ensign had been lowered in a 'Sunset Ceremony', the band would strike up with the National Anthem. This would signal the end of the Reception and prompt our guests to begin making their way home. But this evening there would be no band.

Guests began arriving and we were soon in the thick of it. Any ideas of tape-recorders, gramophones or other sound systems had been discarded, when my husband had an idea. Knowing that one of his Army Intelligence Corps officers had a particularly fine singing voice, he detailed him to take centre stage and commence the singing of 'God save the Queen', on the count of '1, 2, 3' with the promise that we would all join in.

I was very nervous about all this. All the hosting officers and staff were quickly briefed on the arrangement which, thankfully, worked superbly well. I have never heard the National Anthem sung with such gusto.

DAY DREAMING

With a husband away for much of each week displaying with the Red Arrows, there was no hope of a summer holiday that year. Wondering what novelties life might have in store for me, I sat at my sewing machine appliquéing the bright red shape of a Gnat aircraft onto a midnight-blue headscarf. I usually wore this 'supportive' headgear to keep my hair in place on windy days, and it often led to conversations about flying and, of course, the Red Arrows. One of these occasions was at a team social bonding event and, possibly after one drink too many, I found myself declaring that I'd love to learn to fly the Gnat. 'Well,' said this chap, 'why don't you come and try it in the simulator?' Indeed, why not? And on numerous occasions I spent many a happy hour there going through manoeuvres such as wingovers, loops and barrel rolls.

My enthusiasm had obviously been noted, and one grey Saturday I was asked if I would like a flight; it was to be an air test. No prizes for guessing my answer, so two hours later I strode out, appropriately incognito, wearing a flying suit and a bone-dome, prepared for the flight of my life in the gleaming red two-seater trainer, and ready to put my newfound skills into practice.

The Gnat was such a tiny aircraft that you could climb into it without using a ladder. I felt as though I was sitting in the sports car of the aviation world, so close to the ground was I. Otherwise, all the controls, dials and levers in the back seat seemed akin to those of the simulator, which was reassuringly just as it should be. After the necessary flight checks and a gentle ride to the runway came the first excitement of feeling the engine thrumming with power as the aircraft roared off, soon to be followed by sudden pressure on my back and a generally open-mouthed reaction as we accelerated up through the cloud.

Many manoeuvres later, with land, sky, land, more sky flashing past, and not a moment allowed for reflection, came a spell of pure joy. To experience the eerie quiet after the thrusting climb to the top of a loop, then the feeling of weightlessness, followed by the ever-increasing G-force as the Gnat fell seemingly vertically towards the earth, was amazing.

These were sensations like no other in my twenty-three years on this planet, but maybe that was the point – I wasn't on the planet. I was in the air, and it was wonderful, enveloped in the intensely blue sky above the mist of that Saturday morning. Or, was this all a dream …

MEMORIES OF GERMANY

Pink 'NAAFI stamps'.
Ration cards for tea and spirits.
Chips with a large helping of mayonnaise.
Maximum eight cubic metres of personal belongings on an overseas posting.
Petrol coupons.
Maps with all BP garages marked to use said coupons.
The Tick test.
Baby-sitting circle, and precious tokens.
Camouflage settees.
NAAFI Gifts and Durables (or 'Gifts and Gerbils', as the children called it).
The Wegberg Basket, a rota of wives who visited Wegberg Hospital weekly with a basket of stationery and toiletries to give to inpatients from their station.
Long-handled mirrors for IED hunting under your car.
Karnival.
Alte Frau Night, at which ties were chopped off.
Christmas markets and lots of Gluwein.
Temperatures well below minus 20°C.
Shops shutting at mid-day on a Saturday.
Pancake Houses.

Come on, there must be many more!

A DAY IN THE LIFE OF AN RAF WIFE

It can start early, very early. The klaxon, the telephone, is it a Taceval (Tactical Evaluation Exercise) or is it the very, very chilling, 'Sir, sadly I have to notify you that we are now at war …? Or is it a Search and Rescue call-out, such as a night-time rescue of an injured soul on the *Huey Fong* Vietnamese refugee ship out on the South China Sea – no lights, no horizon? Sleep disturbed; action for the man, worry for the wife. An explosion, a gunshot, booming artillery, a coup! Hide in the hallway where there is no outside wall, avoiding stray bullets through the windows. Perhaps an overnight stint at headquarters processing the hapless holidaymakers, dressed only in swimwear, stranded on the beaches obediently following the instructions of BBC World News to await rescue.

Just another night in the life of a military wife. However, on the whole we are left in peace overnight; breakfast as usual, uneventful, a proper start to a normal day?

Later on maybe a coffee morning to bring together old friends and new. A chance to catch up on the news, a time to welcome newcomers, an opportunity for young mums to escape infantile behaviour (of children or husband?) for an hour or two.

Which could lead to a 'girlie lunch' – oh, what a blissful life we really do lead. A meet-up, with a glass (or two) in hand, with special friends, ones who go way back, new ones or those you only meet sporadically when postings coincide.

So many 'out of the ordinary' adventures to reminisce about; the day we went to Lantau Island to give bored and listless refugee children an afternoon of games and fun. Or maybe the day we travelled up into China, quite a novelty in those days. Our experience of the primitive sanitary arrangements, seeing the nursery children, patient and unsquirming on their little chairs awaiting their turn to perform wondrous gymnastics for the visitors.

And so lunchtime is taken care of. Now what about the afternoon? Is it to be an official one, or one of stultifying routine? Is one to dress up or dress down? Meeting royalty or preparing for March Out? Practising a curtsey or scrubbing a floor? Both happen infrequently … but have to be done to a high standard! A military wife has to be flexible.

Evening arrives. Party time! A squadron 'Do', meeting new crew members and wives or a girlfriend in a relaxing atmosphere. A few drinks, a few jokes, a few games? Or maybe it's a 'dressing up' affair, glamorous for the Summer Ball, more formal for the Ladies Guest Night.

Best behaviour, representing your Service, not 'putting your foot in it' (a speciality of mine), supporting my wonderful husband. Yes, my wonderful Royal Air Force husband. On the other hand my evenings could equally be at home on my own ... again!

Lonely? It could be for the new wife; early days, new posting, no military accommodation, no job, no children, no friends yet. It could be very lonely. But not for the wife who makes every effort to show great flexibility and learn from many eclectic experiences. Yes, a day in the life of a military wife is certainly never boring!

LOWERING THE FLAG

The most exciting news for any service wife is that her husband's next tour of duty is to be 'in command' – he's going to be given a station. Exciting – and terrifying. The phrase 'Station Commander's Wife' carries with it equal amounts of pleasurable anticipation and stomach-churning anxiety. It's pay-back time for all those years spent as a loyal camp-follower, moving at short notice from one cheerless married quarter to another. Now you'll be the one living in the Big House and your successful, big-shot husband will be the one giving the orders. But wait: what if everyone hates you? Everyone loved the previous CO's wife and is bound to resent your arrival. How are you going to cope with all that entertaining? What are you going to wear? – because suddenly, every item of clothing in your wardrobe will not bear public scrutiny.

In fact, the reality is somewhere between dreams and nightmares: lots of fun, lots of invitations to events you wouldn't normally be asked to, but far too many duty dinners. Add to that, life in a stunning Lutyens-designed house, depressingly decorated to resemble a cross between *Fawlty Towers* and a care home for retired gentle-folk, so poorly maintained that the attic bedrooms leak. What the allowances give with one hand, they take with the other. But, all-in-all, it is a wonderful experience and you know that, even if your husband is to be promoted further and go on to even greater things, this will be his finest hour.

So it's a cruel blow when fortunes change and you learn the devastating news that the station – 'his' station – is to close. At first the rumours start (never from your husband's lips but invariably from the cleaner) and dire predictions begin to be whispered at the Wives' Club or in the Thrift Shop.

'Have you heard? They're closing us down?'

'No, it can't be. They wouldn't be so stupid. They need us.'

The closure of an RAF station can have an immense impact on the local community and this is especially true of a hospital. When it has provided the highest possible standards of medical care in the area, serving not only military but also NHS patients, its loss is too horrible to contemplate and immediately pressure groups are formed to fight the closure. For the Station Commander's wife this presents a conflict of loyalties which it is impossible to reconcile. The Station Commander has to obey the order he has been given and, however much he may hate that order, however much he may feel that someone has blundered and rail against such stupidity, he has a duty to obey orders and to ensure that the hospital is closed as efficiently and with as much steadying of morale as possible.

His wife, on the other hand, has no such duty to obey orders. So what did I do? I joined the local community in fighting the closure: I wrote to the local papers; I wrote to the national papers; we protested; we organised petitions; we made placards; we marched and we staged sit-ins. Naively, I actually thought that the ground-swell of public opinion against the closure might have made a difference and that I was fighting a winning battle. I really thought that my voice was being heard when, one morning, I received a phone call from the wife of a very senior officer, suggesting that I tone my protests down, as the presence of the CO's wife on the barricades did not look good. It was all heady stuff and I loved it, even though, as I see now, the outcome was inevitable.

Once the final order was signed and the date for closure was fixed, further protest was pointless and my role switched to being one of support for all the wives: not just the wives of the doctors and the medical staff but also of all the cooks, cleaners, drivers and security guards, whether service or civilian. That huge Lutyens-designed house was thrown open to host an endless stream of coffee mornings where people could drop in for a chat to air their anxieties about the future, about redundancy, housing and children's education. And people did drop in. In a way that would have seemed amazing to previous generations of senior officers' wives, any gulf between those living on the officers' patch and those on the airmen's, simply melted away. We were all wives worried about the future, united in our determination to support each other, as the help provided through official channels was never quite enough.

But it wasn't all gloom and doom – we partied on. The date for closure was set for early December but before that we decided to have one last, magnificent summer ball. With suitably black humour, the theme of the ball was to be 'The Titanic'. Just like that glamorous, doomed vessel, mortally wounded below the water-line, we sailed into the sunset, drinking champagne and wearing our finery as we rearranged the deckchairs and the band played on. It was the best summer ball ever.

But winter came and with it the ice. Plans were drawn up for the closing ceremony. I hosted one last luncheon party for all the wives of previous station commanders. It was a very strange occasion which brought home the true extent of the impermanence of a service wife's existence. Seated round the table were all these ladies who had lived in my house before I had, most of them for a longer time than I would, and who knew its delights and drawbacks only too well. It was a bit like having lunch with your husband's ex-mistresses.

Then came the day of the closing ceremony, and nature obliged with a mournful grey sky, a biting wind and the threat of snow. The local TV cameramen arrived and demanded to know where they should set up their equipment. For my husband, one last decision to be made: with lots of very senior RAF officers and hosts of local dignitaries attending, prudence dictated that the ceremony be held in a hangar. It was going to snow and it really wouldn't do to have all those guests sitting in the freezing cold; it would look bad if they all caught pneumonia and died – with no hospital to look after them. The RAF band, muffled up in their greatcoats and wearing those musicians' fingerless gloves, looked anxious as they attempted to keep their instruments in tune – a nice, cosy hangar must have seemed appealing.

But there was no way that this Station Commander was going to suffer the indignity of scaled-down proceedings in a hangar – RAF medics are made of sterner stuff. I suppose we must have shivered on the parade ground, but I really can't remember. All I can remember is the sight of the Station Commander taking the salute for one last time as the flag was lowered and the first flakes of snow fell, and a lone Hercules flew low over the parade ground. Back then, nearly twenty years ago, we had no idea that we would come to associate the Hercules with the sad task of bringing home the dead and injured – and we had little idea just how much a hospital would be needed.

SEARCH AND RESCUE REFLECTIONS

I do hope that, when they look back on their life together, the Duke and Duchess of Cambridge will think that their time at RAF Valley was among the happiest of their life. Valley has given me some of the most precious memories ever and I think of it as a magical time: it was stuck in the middle of nowhere, the winters were hard and we had no money but it was magic.

Thanks to Prince William everyone knows that RAF Valley is home to a Search and Rescue flight. It is also where trainee pilots learn to fly, in our time there on the Hawk which had just come into service. So my husband, fresh from studying for the Diploma in Aviation Medicine, was thrilled to be posted there in his first job as a senior medical officer. He had gone on ahead, leaving me to follow with our children, aged three and fifteen months.

In those days, over thirty years ago, the roads in north Wales were pretty dire and I was dreading the long drive from Farnborough to Anglesey. In order to limit the number of plaintive, 'Are we there yet?' cries, I told a bit of a geographical lie. Wales, I explained, is a big island and we won't be in Wales until we've crossed a huge bridge over the Menai Straits. Be warned that your sins will find you out: when we stopped for a break in Llangollen (that most Welsh of towns and home to the Eisteddfod) our daughter announced to everyone in the cafe, 'We are going to Wales.' Pitying looks all round from the locals whose feelings of contempt for ignorant English tourists were reinforced.

Anglesey, Ynys Mon in Welsh, is itself pretty remote and Valley even more so, situated on the far west of the island, surrounded by open farmland and stunning beaches. Our time there was a time of contrasts: we had, as I said, no money – no one relying on the military salary did – and there were some flying officer pilots on income support. Despite being married to a highly qualified doctor, I had a very tight house-keeping budget but what I remember is the abundance of blackberries in the hedgerows all round Valley; the wonderful Welsh lamb from the local farm; field mushrooms and my first taste of wild samphire, picked from rocky cliffs near the beaches.

It was a politically sensitive time, when militant Welsh nationalists were torching the holiday homes of English tourists and Welsh was spoken aggressively in shops by people who would be speaking English until a visitor appeared. I tried to learn some Welsh but it defeated me, other than to leave me with a love of hearing it sung and a propensity to cry whenever I hear 'Men of Harlech'. We were hardly aware of any hostility and only ever received a warm welcome from everyone who lived nearby. This was partly due to our friendship with the 22 Squadron flight commander, whose Welsh credentials were impeccable, and also to the fact that Valley's medics were closely involved with Search and Rescue, working alongside both the RAF and local Mountain Rescue teams. We were totally integrated with the local community and my children, although they were too young to realise it, were learning their first lesson in being a community within a community; dimly aware that there was a culture and a language outside the station boundary that was different from theirs and enriched their lives. Our daughter's first school was Ysgol Babanod Y Tywyn (where every one of the teachers was called 'Miss Williams') and she learned to count up to ten in Welsh – a skill which has stood her in good stead ever since!

They also learned that Daddy did not have a nine-to-five job and that he could be called out, often in the middle of the night, and might not be back next morning before school or nursery, meaning that they left home with that feeling of uncertainty that every Service child grows up with, a mixture of pride and resentment – a knowledge, gradually acquired, that their life was different from that of their civilian friends. It was at Valley that my children first became vaguely aware of what life in the Royal Air Force meant for them; it was at Valley that they made their first real friends and said their first 'goodbyes' when postings dragged friends apart; it was at Valley that I realised the enormity of the role of a service wife.

Winters on Anglesey were hard, with storm force winds battering the island for weeks on end, whipping up huge seas all round the coast. The SAR flight was on standby to assist the lifeboats and it seemed as though the phone rang every night. My husband would be out of bed before the second ring. Unlike the aircrew, he slept at home as he was also on call for the Station Practice. He would struggle into his immersion suit, which lived in the spare room to save time, and both frightened and fascinated our small son. Then he would hurl himself into the medical centre's mini and race down to the squadron where the Wessex would be ready to go, rotor blades already turning. After he left, the house always felt empty for a moment. Then two sleepy children would appear, clutching teddies, and creep into bed beside me.

'Has Daddy been called out?'

'Yes, don't worry. Back soon. Snuggle down and go to sleep.'

As they burrowed down under the duvet, we made up a story for the rescue. A pirate ship was the favourite to be rescued and the very best story of all was when Daddy was winched onto the deck of *The Black Pig* to save Captain Pugwash from a watery grave. But however the story unfolded, it always had the same ending: just as the ship is sinking beneath the waves, the big yellow Wessex looms out of a dark sky.

'Hooray!' they all cry. 'We're saved thanks to 22 Squadron.'

And so the children became aware of their world expanding: nursery school, big school, the medical centre, 22 Squadron, RAF Valley, Anglesey, Snowdonia – and beyond that, the whole wild world. Our next posting took us to the other side of the world, to Hong Kong, but it was at RAF Valley I think that we first became properly aware that we were a Service family with all the problems and all the privileges that that entails.

THEY MIGHT HAVE TOLD US

> Do any wives know what we're in for
> On the glorious day we get wed?
> We're sure it will be so romantic
> And find an assault course, instead.
>
> It seems an exciting adventure,
> We'll travel the world, oh what fun,
> Far-flung and exotic, but sadly,
> For most it's around the A1!
>
> We had no idea of the 'March Out'
> And the mad things a wife's needed for,
> Like reversing on knees in the kitchen
> And scrubbing towards the back door.

FINAL REFLECTIONS

And when we are flopped in our rollers
And dressed in our scruffiest gear
At happy hour (nice peaceful evening)
He brings the chaps back for more beer!

At dining-in nights we're abandoned
To cope as we always have done
And next day we hear of the antics
And wish we'd have seen all the fun.

Yes, a wife has a lot to put up with
Supporting her man through it all
And then there's the ominous visit
When a senior wife comes to call.

She stands on the doorstep, quite flustered,
There's a desperate look in her eye
And she's asking, 'Will you run the Wives' Club?'
And you just can't say 'No' (though you try).

We had no idea we'd be tested
– our fortitude, patience, the lot
And our halos are definitely gleaming
For a 'dead easy' ride this is not.

We dutifully cope with the drawbacks
When we thought we'd be having a ball,
But if we had known – if they'd TOLD us –
We wouldn't have changed it ... at all.

About the charities supported by this book

The editors believe sincerely in the work carried out by RAF charities and have decided to support the Royal Air Forces Association and the Royal Air Force Benevolent Fund.

For many years RAF charities have provided comfort, succour and support for any member of the RAF family, whenever and whatever the need. RAF personnel and their families dedicate their lives to their country; these charities have a mission to ensure that the sacrifice made by RAF personnel and families does not involve suffering, poverty or loneliness.

Support provided by the charities is available to serving personnel past or present, and their families. It covers a wide range, from visits and short breaks to offering practical advice in matters financial or emotional as well as social support to families. Both charities also run appropriate care and respite homes. All these facilities are available in times of difficulty for recipients irrespective of the cause of the need, their rank or relationship to the original member of the Royal Air Force.

The charities work very closely together and provide fundraising through membership in the case of the Association or direct giving through the offices of the Benevolent Fund. The charities run many initiatives designed to bring families closer and offer comfort in times of separation or other need. They seek to help any member of the RAF family and their dependants, both during and after active service.

Collectively, these charities spend close to £30m a year on the needs of their recipients and this work is completely funded by the generosity of either members or benefactors' vital donations. Neither charity receives government contributions to their work on behalf of the RAF family.

The RAF family is large, with reputedly over one million members who are eligible to receive help. Many are too proud or unaware of the benefits that may be available to them when they are faced with a wide range of issues from childcare, relationship difficulties and debt, to injury, disability, illness and bereavement. More recently, the charities have identified major youth work projects to provide access to quality facilities and activities in order to relieve the strain on RAF parents and to recognise the importance of the RAF Cadet Movement, which is nearly 55,000 strong.

To find out more, please visit *www.rafbf.org* and *www.rafa.org.uk*